G000065849

Looking Back

A Century of Life in Bethnal Green

Joyce Hampton

not just
another book

not just
another book

First Published in 2015 by: Rainbow Valley Books

Second Edition in 2016 by: not just another book

(For Joyce Hampton email)
hampton.joyce14@yahoo.com

Illustrations provided by The Author
Cover Design Joyce Hampton
Main Text Set in Times New Roman 12.0

Published by: not just another book
ISBN: 978-0-9935665-0-9

Printed and bound by Berforts Limited

For

Evie, Alice and Myles, with the love of a proud Nanna to her three adored grandchildren. I hope you will read this book as you grow older and be very proud of this part of your roots too.

...

My wonderful husband John

...

and Zoe

(Our faithful Cairn terrier)

Contents

Acknowledgements

This book has been a journey of learning for me about an area I knew only a little about. But from curiosity comes learning and with this knowledge I have become so very proud of my roots.

First of all I would like to acknowledge my husband, John, without whose encouragement this book would never have been completed. I will always be in his debt for all the advice he has given me and for all the many trips he made with me to London to take photos and research the area. In particular I would like to thank him for the time he has given to guide me through some areas of research, especially the history of World War Two about which he has a great depth of knowledge and finally the many hours he has spent diligently proof-reading various drafts of this book.

My gratitude to those sadly departed relatives who patiently imparted to me many of the everyday family-life memories included in this book, and also (and by no means least) my grateful thanks to my mother, Mrs Vera Overy, for ensuring that some of the family information for which I had incomplete details was correct – for a 94 year old her memory is remarkable.

I should like to give a special thanks to the wonderful staff at Tower Hamlets Archive in Bancroft Road and to Bethnal Green Library for all their patience, help and assistance without which many details of this book would never have come to light.

The *Stairway to Heaven Memorial Trust* deserves a very special mention, especially Sandra who works tirelessly to raise funds to complete a long overdue memorial to the many souls lost in the Bethnal Green Tube disaster. Her encouragement and assistance have been so valuable to this book. Any contributions to the Memorial Trust would, I am sure, be gratefully received.

Please go to www.stairwaytoheavenmemorial.org to read further details about the project and to donate funds.

I would also like to acknowledge the invaluable assistance given by Stephen Sanders who provided many wonderful family anecdotes, as did my cousins Gloria Parker and Janice Drewett with their various insights into childhood experiences growing up in Bethnal Green – together with those of my cousin Sheila Crates – who unwittingly inspired me to write this book

I would also like to give thanks to Barton, one of the current occupants of 49 Approach Road, for his hospitality, kindness and help. Adam Neczaj also deserves a mention for all his unstinting IT support – without this, the book may well have remained unfinished.

I am indebted to Finian Lynch and Hayley Harper for their input into the marketing of this and future books as well as their advice on this second edition.

Hayley Harper also deserves a special mention for all her input into the beautiful and eye catching new book cover.

Finally, I should like to thank my friends Barbara and Pam for their kindness, advice and input. As one-time local girls, their memories are invaluable in re-telling some of the events that are part of Bethnal Green's story.

FOREWORD

Bethnal Green has had a long, varied, often colourful history, but certainly never dull! My father's family hails from this part of London and were always proud of their roots. As a child I loved to hear from various family members recollections of their lives which, over the years, were lovingly noted down. Sections of this book rely heavily on those notes and family oral tradition as primary source material. I have no reason to doubt its accuracy. Certainly the family traditions seem to match each period of social history. The extended family, its friends and the local environment, are inextricably entwined, as the book develops.

A fond pastime of my relatives was to try to remember as much as possible, then relay their memories to me as if they were sure I would not forget them nor their way of life. The period of time they lived through was one of great change and development, many discoveries were made that today we take for granted but each were a miracle to our ancestors – for example: street lighting, penicillin, radios and electricity in the home. They lived through two world wars and saw many changes to working class life including the abolition of the Workhouse. I hope the anecdotal information from various family members will give my book an added dimension to everyday life in Bethnal Green.

This book is not a family history but a history of life in Bethnal Green with family and friends recollections woven into the history. Starting in 1862 with a family birth, the story then takes the reader through to 1962 by which time the family had moved on to various locations both within London and further afield. Occasionally an event is recorded in the book that took place outside the Bethnal Green boundaries but as the event had an impact on the history of Bethnal Green

I have included it. Some events were international but nonetheless affected Bethnal Green therefore they are also included.

During research I was pleased to find that everyone I have spoken to, either resident or past resident, are proud of their roots – but are fed up with the comparison to the 'soap' Eastenders or salacious tales of the Krays. They are all keen for a more balanced view of life in Bethnal Green. To this end the book is meant to be a history with a difference – proper historical facts, i.e. the bones of events international, national and local to the area (sometimes a little out of the area) and then layered with the flesh of emotions from real people past and present living in the area. This obviously includes a great deal from my family history which I noted down from a very young age, plus extended family and friends and then people I have recently met who have given me some further details.

Bethnal Green is part of the area known as London's *East End* – the mere mention of which conjures up scenes of slums, disease, poverty and overcrowding but that is to only look at snapshots of life in the 19th Century. There was and *is* much more to the story of Bethnal Green and for those who lived in the area, and Bethnal Green descendants, as mentioned above, deplore the type-casting of their ancestors.

All the family knew that not far from where they lived there was great poverty. They did witness bare foot and barelegged children dressed in ill-fitting garments, which was often the lot of children whose parents were unable to find regular work. Many a man living in Bethnal Green would stand day after day at a dock or factory gate waiting anxiously to see if he would be lucky enough to be chosen for a day's work – no prospects – just a hand to mouth existence for himself and his family.

The wider history of the area can be traced back to Roman times but when the Saxons in the 7th Century sailed up the

Thames to the abandoned Roman settlement of Londinium they started to settle east of London. It is possible that each settlement was named for the Saxon leader, hence 'Blida' gave his name to the area now known as Bethnal Green; however, Bethnal Green is first mentioned in a 13th Century property deed where it is referred to as 'Blithehall' which may be an amalgam of two Anglo-Saxon words: *blithe* meaning 'happy' and *haelth* meaning 'angle, corner or nook'. Whatever the origin of the name, what is certain is that the first settlement was on the current-day site of the Bethnal Green Museum of Childhood. Behind this settlement could be found St Winifred's Well from where the locals would draw their water each day.

During the medieval period, the original settlement was little more than a village with common land at the centre linked by several roads to the walled City of London and other settlements. The village grew and, as time went by, many fine town houses were built to accommodate the gentry from the City of London. Geoffrey Chaucer was a frequent visitor to the area; he was employed by the King and for many years lived in lodgings above Aldgate from where he witnessed the Peasants' Revolt of 1381. Samuel Pepys, with many friends who lived in the fine town houses thereabouts, was another frequent visitor and recommended the good cream, strawberries and cherries to be found in Bethnal Green.

Bethnal Green became famous with the legend of the ballad of the blind beggar. The ballad tells of a blinded soldier named Henry Montfort, the son of the famous knight Simon de Montfort, killed at the battle of Evesham in 1265. The ballad tells how Henry was badly wounded and blinded during this battle and found wandering amongst the dead and dying on the battlefield by a young nobleman's daughter who gave him shelter and compassionately nursed him back to health. Gradually the couple fell in love and eventually married. Their marriage was blessed with a daughter Besse who, in time, grew into an attractive young woman. Although Besse was beautiful she could not find a husband because of her father's apparent poverty. Besse was courted by four suitors; a rich gentleman, a knight, a London Merchant and an innkeeper's son, but each withdrew their courtship when they met her father in his shabby garb that is except for the Knight who had fallen deeply in love with Besse and was willing to forego a reasonable dowry in order to marry her. The Knight asked for her hand in marriage and her father not only consented but gave the happy couple a dowry of £3,000 and an additional £100 for Besse's wedding dress.

The official guide of Bethnal Green quotes this charming poem of the legend:

> *He was a blind beggar that had lost his sight and*
> *he had a daughter most pleasant and bright and*
> *many a gallant, brave suitor had she*
> *for none were as comely as pretty Besse*
>
> *but though she was of favour most fair yet*
> *seeing she was but a beggar's heir of*
> *ancient housekeepers despised was she*
> *whose sons came as suitors to pretty Besse.*

The original borough emblem of Bethnal Green (prior to Bethnal Green eventually being merged into the newly formed Tower Hamlets) was an escutcheon edged with *The Borough of Bethnal Green* and a picture in the centre supposedly of the blind beggar and his beautiful daughter. St Matthew's Church also took *The Blind Beggar* as an emblem.

The Great Fire of London broke out in 1666 and Samuel Pepys recorded in his diaries that he and several other prosperous people sent their money and plate to Bethnal

Green, placing it in the home of William Ryder, for safe keeping. When the City of London was rebuilt many of the bricks used in the construction were made in Bethnal Green from clay dug from the area now known as Brick Lane. The Fire of London caused a rethink of building regulations thus making buildings within the City much more expensive to construct. Therefore accommodation that was not subject to these strict new regulations, i.e. *outside the city walls,* was cheaper to build, thus more attractive to buy or rent.

Towards the end of the 17th Century the village of Bethnal Green expanded as immigrants left their home shores, mainly for religious reasons, to settle in England. After the revocation of the Edict of Nantes in 1685 a great wave of Huguenots fled France in search of religious freedom, my own ancestors included. In this period an increased building of accommodation began to alleviate the overcrowding in the Spitalfields area of London and this certainly began to change Bethnal Green from a rural community to an urban area.

The Huguenots were, for a while, a very influential section of society. Many of them were well educated and had gained professional skills as doctors, bankers, clock makers and silversmiths. There was also a large contingent of silk weavers amongst their number who were enthusiastically welcomed and encouraged to settle here for their skills in producing such luxurious fashionable cloth – even King James I encouraged their skills in 1608, by planting Mulberry trees, essential for silk production. Sadly the wrong type of mulberries were planted!

These immigrants were influential in changing the landscape of the area, many affluent Huguenots built fine three-storey houses, some of which can still be seen today – for example, in Fournier Street. Less affluent Huguenots also left their mark by building modest weavers' cottages with little gardens; the Huguenots had a great love of flowers and birds. In 1826 the law regulating silk imports was replaced with a customs duty, allowing many cheap foreign imports to flood the market. The silk weaving industry went into steep financial decline for the weavers who, in order to survive, now found themselves working very long hours for minimal return.

In the fast changing world we live in, to look back over the events of a century is to look back at another world entirely, although I hope people's attitudes to life and how they relate to each other has not changed that much, the challenges are different, the principles the same. So let us go to the start of this one hundred year journey...

Looking Back

A Century of Life in Bethnal Green

1

Life in the Victorian Era

The year is 1862 and on the 29 January in a little terraced house in Ann's Place, Bethnal Green, a baby girl has just been born to Susannah and John Harris. The couple already have four sons and the birth of their daughter will complete their family.

Ann's Place was a single row of houses in Pritchard's Road with a thin pavement edging the front of this little row of properties with a narrow cobbled road beyond. The road was named by Andrew Pritchard, a tile-maker from Hackney who had purchased the land, part of a twenty-acre farm, in 1813. Mr Pritchard named several roads he built in the area after members of his family hence Ann's Place, Andrew's Road, Marian Square and Emma Street to name but a few. Although there is no record of the actual date of construction Ann's Place had first appeared on the 1819 Laurie and Whittles map. The properties in Ann's Place were very small two-storey brick-built terraced houses, inside was dark with only one single sash window front and back per floor to let any natural light into the rooms. Apart from the two up two down rooms of the house there was a 'privy' outside in the small yard at the rear of the house. Nearby in the street was a communal pump for fresh water. The only other light would have been from the small half-moon fanlight above the solid wooden front door. The early occupants were not wealthy.

Poverty was a great demon which many fought but were unable to overcome. With minimal nourishment, poor sanitation and frequent bouts of disease such as typhus, tuberculosis and cholera the casualty list was inevitably high. In 1866, another cholera outbreak claimed many more lives, some of which might have been saved had there been hospitals other than those within the local Workhouse. A peoples' dispensary – Queen Adelaide's – opened in 1866 on the corner of Pollards Row, then two hospitals were built – The Mildmay Mission Hospital in Hackney Road with three 10-bed wards for men, women and children and a Medical Mission in Turville Street.

Thomas John Barnardo came to work at the London Hospital in 1867 and witnessed at first hand the destitution that the cholera epidemic left in its wake with hundreds of orphans sleeping rough and forced to either beg for their food or work in factories. Life could be cruel at times as illustrated by two contemporary reports in *The Bethnal Green Times:*

The Homeless Poor - 2 February 1867
(relating to the untimely death of Thomas
Hawkins aged 2 ½ years old)

His mother, Mary Hawkins, had been homeless since her husband had left her two years previously. She was an artificial flower maker by trade but for the past 15 months she had not found employment. She resorted to selling cigar lights in the streets with her elder son. When night came they would usually go to the Casual ward of the Workhouse to sleep. They depended on the morning and evening meal provided at the Casual ward for food and the mother stated at her child's inquest that they never begged and she had never taken her little child out into the snow in order to win compassion from passers-by.

> *Death from starvation in Bethnal Green - 20 July*
> *1867 (refers to Edward Harrison who was found*
> *apparently dying in Church Street)*
> *...witnesses to his collapse hailed a cab to take him*
> *to the Workhouse but he died shortly after arrival.*
> *His sister, who was called upon to identify him,*
> *said he had been the occupier of a small chandler*
> *shop but recently had become homeless and*
> *without any means of support. His sister had*
> *provided him with 5 shillings a week to help him.*

Inside the houses in Ann's Place as in the surrounding area there was neither electricity nor running water. An Act of Parliament in the early 19th Century had set up the East London Waterworks Company for the purpose of drawing water from the River Lea and to build waterworks and reservoirs at Old Ford: however, due to the rapid increase of accommodation in the area not all premises were connected to the supply and those that were often only had access three times a week. Sewerage removal was not properly undertaken until the mid-19th Century but, even when this service became compulsory, not many properties were connected to the system.

Many properties in Bethnal Green were, at this time, occupied by more than one family. The overcrowded conditions often led to high infant mortality with many adults not living beyond what would now be termed middle-age. There were many reasons for such high death rates, one of which was The Regents Canal (built 1820) that ran nearby and had been attributed as being the source of a cholera outbreak in 1848 in Pritchard's Road. The conditions of both the canal and its banks were often dire. In fact, the filth left on the banks of the canal was also blamed for outbreaks of other water-borne diseases such as typhus.

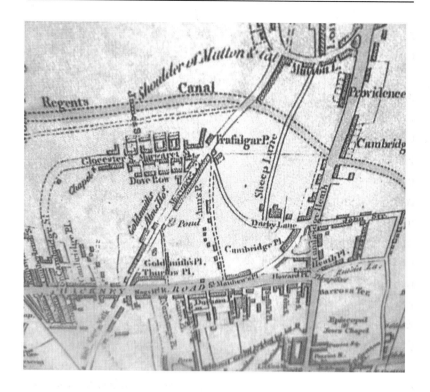

Map with Ann's Place in the centre. The Regents Canal (built 1820) that ran nearby was attributed as being the source of a cholera outbreak in 1848

Susannah lit the sparsely furnished rooms with candles once it became dark; coal or wood were burned to warm the house and to cook. The couple both worked hard to provide for their family but it was difficult at times as work was not always as regular as they would have wished. Susannah worked at home sewing petticoats while John went out to work as a labourer nearby.

During 1860, a treaty of commerce between Great Britain and France allowing the importation of duty-free French silk was signed, sounding the death knell to the jobs of many silk weavers residing in Bethnal Green and Spitalfields. Desperate for work, they searched for employment in the Docks or became part of the growing rag trade often working from home or in 'sweat-shops' producing cheap ready-to wear clothes.

In 1862, through the encouragement of Charles Dickens, Angela Burdett-Coutts built nearby the U-shaped Columbia Dwellings. They were of several storeys with a three-storey Gothic arch built into the brickwork of the central section. Each block contained 45 apartments and each apartment consisted of two-roomed family accommodation; the living room was approximately twelve feet by ten feet and contained a boiler and oven whilst the bedroom (in which the whole family would sleep) was twelve feet by eight feet. Gas and running water were installed and a superintendent and two porters were employed to clean the communal areas. The top floor of each block was reserved as a laundry and drying space for the tenants. The building, together with the impressive Columbia Road Market, was demolished in 1958.

Tragedy struck when Susannah became ill and suddenly died leaving four young sons and her little daughter Susannah, just two years old at the time of mother's death. Too young to be left on her own while her father went out to work, Susannah went to live in nearby Gibraltar Walk with her grandmother Annie Taylor. Her older brothers attended school where they received an education before going on to earn a living in various trades but girls in that era were rarely given the opportunity to be educated so sadly Susannah was never able to read or write.

It was not until 1870 that the first Education Act became law – the very first piece of legislation to deal specifically with providing education across Britain. The Act allowed Voluntary schools to carry on unchanged but established a system of 'school boards' to build and manage schools in areas where they were needed. The boards were locally elected bodies funded from the local rates. Unlike the 'Voluntary' schools, religious teaching in the board schools was to be 'non-denominational'.

Gas lighting of the streets of Bethnal Green had begun approximately two decades before but by 1872, 800 gas lamps lit the streets until a strike by the Amalgamated Society of Gasmen seeking shorter working hours plunged the streets into darkness. The owners were pressured into resolving this issue which they did by charging the ringleaders with conspiracy and recruiting replacement labour.

The 1876 Royal Commission on the Factory Acts suggested education should become compulsory in order to stop child labour. Then, in 1880, a further Act – The Elementary Education Act – finally made school attendance compulsory between the ages of 5 and 10. Many children worked outside school hours and truancy was a major issue because not all parents could afford to give up income earned by their children, especially in poor and deprived areas such as Bethnal Green.

Susannah had first started work as a 6 year old child, helping her grandmother make infant footwear. The grim reality of children working from such a young age was not unusual at that time[1] – it was often necessary so that the family might earn enough to provide sustenance for all. This was a time long before Government introduced the child benefit scheme – known as the Family Allowance – and even a little pair of hands would be put to good use to help provide the family with enough money to survive. Susannah was a loving[2] child who adored her grandmother, father and brothers.

---

[1] This social phenomenon of large numbers of children forming a family's income source, and ultimately an insurance for the parents in later life is echoed today in Third World Countries.

[2] Susannah was very close to her daughter Lydie and she told me how she had asked about her mum's life and family. Susannah herself said she loved her family very much and Lydie recalled her mother as being a loving and kind lady. Several

Many families in the poorer areas of the district lived in cramped conditions with inadequate sanitation. As the 19th Century progressed, the area had undergone an immense change. Where once a rural setting had met the eye, the industrial revolution had arrived and with it the growth of urbanisation. Terraced houses started to spring up, basic, cheaply built with bricks made from the local London clay found in great quantities in the vicinity of Brick Lane. As the century progressed, and with the arrival of fresh waves of immigrants, even wooden sheds in the gardens of the weavers' cottages were utilised for much needed accommodation without consideration to suitability.

Often whole families would be involved in working in a trade from home, such as tailoring; the tailor might occupy the only chair the family possessed while the rest of the family sat on the bare boards of the floor or possibly a mattress, remaining there for hours on end diligently working almost without a break to stretch cramped limbs. A harsh existence indeed at times in the Victoria era – even a young child would be required to work long hours. In a room that was only dimly lit by candle, bending close to the work trying to concentrate on the task, fingers numb and stiff from long hours plying a needle, eyes straining and watering from the poor light, life was grim for all. Other trades were undertaken by families at home such as clothes peg production, and matchbox or boot box assembly.

In a report by Charles Booth produced in 1889, *Life and Labour of the People*, one of the team he had led, investigating poverty in London, was his cousin Beatrice Potter who noted in a chapter of the report:

---

of my asides and descriptions of my family members are based on such direct anecdotal evidence.

In this quarter thirty or forty thousand Jews of all nationalities and from all countries congregate, and form in the midst of our cosmopolitan metropolis a compact Jewish community.

Jewdisch is a language of the streets, and Hebrew characters are common in shop windows and over doorways. Overcrowding in all its forms, whether in the close packing of human beings within four walls, or in the filling up of every available building space with dwellings and workshops is the distinguishing mark of the district.[3]

With long hours spent working, not much time was left for housework or for more than a cursory nod to personal hygiene but this is not to say that all families lived in squalor. Hygiene standards were nowhere near as high as they are today, but following an Act of Parliament to encourage boroughs to provide facilities, a bath-house had been built in Cheshire Street in 1898. Personal washing usually meant a bowl with cold water but the advent of bath-houses, which became an essential public service during this period, meant that hygiene standards could be greatly improved as many Londoners still lived in crowded homes with no internal water supply. Bath-houses remained in popular use until well into the 20th Century. Often mothers would sell their hair in order to buy food for their children but would labour long in washing both children and clothing in order to provide a certain standard of cleanliness.

---

[3] How similar to our present 'cosmopolitan' country where some areas reflect the culture of Islamic and other immigrating communities.

A recent photo of the Cheshire Street bath house building

Before moving on from this subject, I feel I should bring to the reader's attention another famous bathing emporium – the Russian Vapour Baths – the most famous of which was Schewzik's of 86 Brick Lane. This form of bathing, brought to East London by Jewish refugees, particularly from Eastern Europe, was derived from the old Russian Banyas.

On a visit to Schewzik's, once you had paid your admission fee, you would be given a key to a locker to store your clothes in. After you had stripped off your clothing you would enter a communal room where you were given a basin to fill with hot water and, using your own soap, you would scrub and rinse yourself clean. From this room you would go to a 'Hot' room, and once you were acclimatised to the heat you would move onto the *really* hot room. While in this room you would beat yourself all over with a besom broom to increase your circulation.

A further even hotter room awaited you before you headed for the shower room – the water there was ice cold. This method of bathing required you to repeat the process in order to gain total cleanliness. It was also purported to give 'relief to sufferers of rheumatics, gout, sciatica etc.'

In spite of many people attaining cleanliness, the Victorians' view of Bethnal Green was one of total deprivation, with the local population being seen as uneducated, unwashed and uncouth. Many well-heeled and well intentioned people felt a desire to 'improve the lot' of these people. A pamphlet written in 1888 by Congregational Ministers, *The Bitter Cry of Outcast London,* shocked people with its stark description of poverty, overcrowding, disease and despair often leading to suicide in many parts of East London. Part of the report describes accommodation as being insanitary with often two families sharing cramped living space. A sanitary inspector reported finding in a cellar a father, mother, three small children and four pigs! In another room a man was found suffering from smallpox while his wife lay recovering from her eighth confinement.

Although there was great poverty and deprivation in areas of Bethnal Green (poverty was acute in the 'town' part of Bethnal Green rather than nearer to the 'Green' itself), it must be said there were residents living in Bethnal Green who were above the poverty line, earning a regular wage and were therefore able to enjoy a reasonable standard of living.

Even so, not all children who lost a parent or, worse, both parents, were cared for by kindly relatives. Many children could be found struggling to survive on the streets. Charles Dickens, a great champion of these children, had been born into a middle-class family but when he was only 12 years old his father had been taken to Debtors' Prison. The young Dickens' experience of having to work very long hours to support himself moulded his future outlook on life. When he grew into an adult, he embarked on a writing career and brought the plight of the poor (especially the children) to the notice of the upper classes. One of his great friends was Angela Burdett Coutts – the great philanthropist, whose championing of the poor will be touched on in greater detail in a later chapter.

The first 'Children's Home' was founded in 1868, by a Methodist minister, Thomas Bowman Stephenson, who had been greatly affected by the plight and often sad fate of street children in London. The first home was a renovated stable in Church Street, Waterloo, and the first admissions were two boys on 9 July 1869. In 1871 the home was moved to Bonner Road, Bethnal Green, where girls were also admitted. Some of these little children went onto fame and fortune. One such was admitted on 24 February 1898, his name was Walter Tull, who later became a

very famous footballer. Walter Tull was also the first British born black officer in the British Army. He joined the Army early in the war serving in the 'Footballers' Battalions of the Middlesex Regiment. He was promoted to sergeant and in 1917 was commissioned as a second-lieutenant. Following action in Italy he was recommended for a Military Cross. He returned to Northern France only to be killed on 25 March 1918 during the Spring Offensive. His body was never found.

As the scale of the orphaned and abandoned children became more apparent, so more homes in other parts of London and further afield were opened. All the homes caring for these children also gave each child the basic skills to earn their living in various trades such as carpentry, printing and domestic help. On 15 June 1915, the last evening hymn at the

Children's Home was sung in the Home's Chapel before the premises were closed and the remaining children were moved to the Harpenden site.

2

Working life, Housing Conditions and the Workhouse

Susannah Harris grew into an adult earning her living working alongside her grandmother as an infant bootmaker. Not far from Susannah's family home lived the Norton family. James Norton had been born in 1860, the second son of Alfred and Margaret Norton. As a young man, he was a keen cyclist and an amateur boxer in his spare time. He was a member of the Oxford House Boys' Club in Bethnal Green and represented the club in several events. Oxford House was an important part of life for the young men of the area and a great range of community work was carried out by volunteers.

Various family members have all described young Susannah as having a 'bright intellect, of a lively disposition, a caring, kindly and patient soul' who would offer help to anyone; she did not have a lot herself but would give whatever she could to someone whose need was greater than hers. She was small of stature, with bright brown eyes, brown hair and a kindly soft voice. I mention these family recollections of a local girl, who was to become my own great grandmother, as she was typical of her time and place. This is an echo of fact that the bulk of the residents of Bethnal Green or indeed of East London as a whole were not of the lowest orders, as is often suggested with such relish in books about the area.

James and Susannah started their married life in Fournier Street, Spitalfields – where on 7 May 1889, their first child,

James was a type setter for a newspaper in Fleet Street when, at the age of 21, he married Susannah Lucy Harris on 5 June 1885; at that time it was rare to have a wedding photo of the happy couple but sometimes a studio photo would be taken to record the happy event and such a photo was taken of James and Susannah.

Maggie (my grandmother) was born - she was followed by James (1891), Lydie (1893), Elizabeth (1896) and finally Charlotte (1899). By the time their last child was born, the family had moved to 20 Thorold Street. Couples often had large families in that era, birth control was limited, infant mortality high and there was a need for the potential income from a family having several children.

James was said to be an honest, quiet, family man, beloved and respected by all his family. He was of medium build with brown eyes and brown hair that turned to a steely silver grey in later years but his hair never receded. He worked hard to provide for his growing family.

Spitalfields and its neighbour Bethnal Green were highly populated areas with larger numbers of families living there that could lay claim to Huguenot descent – many streets were filled with tall narrow town-house style terraces whose top floor had been given over to be used as a workshop with long, deep windows to enable the weavers to gain as much natural working light as possible.

When Charles Booth produced his report in 1889, he included the long weekly working hours in trades favoured by the people of Bethnal Green, such as French polishing (55 ½ hours), market porters (72 hours) and railway car men (84 hours). At that time there was no legislation to limit working hours.

In 1884, The Reform Act (known as the Third Reform Act) following on from the earlier Reform Acts of 1832 and 1867 was entered onto the Statute Book, this gave the right to vote to all adult males who either owned or occupied premises valued at or above £10 per annum. This meant that if you were over 21 years of age and in regular employment and even if your home was rented by you then you could, in theory, have a say in government, an immense stride forward in democracy as now up to 90% of the local male population could qualify to vote. This did not mean there were no anomalies to the system, many who appeared on the register in the early years did not in strictness have the right to vote. Bethnal Green residents voting after 1885 in General Elections were voting predominantly Liberal – which was the effective 'left' wing of the day.

The Bethnal Green area had undergone immense change during the 19th Century and by the end of the century it had become grossly overcrowded. In 1900, the Old Nichol Street Rookery was demolished and in its place arose the Boundary Estate (thus named as it was built at the boundary with Shoreditch). This estate was the first council housing estate in the world. Two later famous residents of this estate were brothers – Lew Grade and Bernard Delfont who grew up there.

In 1909, the Bethnal Green Estate was built with money bequeathed by the philanthropist, William Richard Sutton, to provide dwellings and houses for the poor of London and other towns and cities in England.

The Nortons may not have been very affluent but they were a happy family and all the children attended school.

On one occasion the children were taken to the local photographer for a family photo. We take photos for granted nowadays but then it was still quite a novel and rare event.

James as a youth, in the back row on the right hand side of my grandmother (Maggie) with Lydie in front of him, Charlotte (Lottie) to her left and Elizabeth (Lizzie) in front of Maggie. Photograph c. 1904

Lydie wrote articles for a local newspaper in the 1970s and here she recalls of her childhood in 1904:

Then and Now

I was about 11 years old and it was a bank holiday Monday. My friend and I planned to take our young brothers and sisters to spend the day by the River Lea. We were a party of six and we set off with sandwiches, cakes and sweets. We took return tickets on the tram and had quite an enjoyable time on the top deck, singing all the way.

We had rides on the roundabout and swings as well as donkey rides. At that time things were only a penny a go, so a few coppers (old pennies) went a long way. We spent a very happy time together; the only time we rested was when we sat on the grass to eat our food. Then we played games and got very tired, so we decided to take a boat trip before starting for home.

We took our turn in the queue to wait for a boat. After a while we managed to get on one and were all very pleased until my friend's little brother said he didn't like it and burst into tears. He would not stop crying and we did not know how to pacify him, so we told him we would give him the purse to hold if he would stop crying. This worked for a few minutes but then he threw the purse into the water! The purse sank like a stone with the few coppers we had left and our return tickets.

We got off the boat and had quite a long walk along the tow-path before we reached Leabridge Road, the start of our journey home. I think it was at this point about 3 miles from Bethnal Green, but it felt like 33 miles to us. I can't remember how long it took us as we took it in turns to carry the two 3 year olds and we had to stop many times to rest.

James and Susannah's son James became a printer's assistant, due no doubt to the influence of his father. In that period, and for many years after, to get employment 'in the print' you had to be recommended either by a friend or family member already in the printing world. The girls took up various semi-skilled employments. Again, Lydie provided witness, when she wrote:

Then and Now

I *left school in 1907 at the age of 14 years. I went to work in a box-making factory, where my wages were 2s 6d (12 ½ p) per week. I made reasonable progress, and after a year I was put onto piece-work. It was very hard going, but I managed to earn 10s (50p) or 12s (60p) a week, which was good money in those days for a 15 year old girl.*

The working hours were from 8am to 8pm Monday to Friday and 8am to 2pm on Saturdays. We had one hour for dinner-break and half an hour for tea break. We had just 10 minutes lunch-break on Saturdays. We never got paid for any bank holidays and a week's holiday with pay was right out of the question. We were allowed to be late no more than three minutes in the morning, then after that we were shut out for half a day. There wasn't a canteen and the tea was made in beer cans.

But what a difference today! A girl can go straight from school at sixteen to learn a trade and get £20 a week or more. She gets all Bank holidays and at least two weeks holiday in the summer – all with pay, Most firms have a canteen and quite a number give luncheon vouchers. The hours are usually 8:30 am to 4pm for five working days. I never thought I would live to see such a great change in working conditions.

Lydie also wrote another short article in which she describes life as a young girl before the advent of Social Services:

> ### *Then and Now*
> *As a young girl I always had a soft feeling towards elderly people. I used to feel very sad when I saw then coming from the workhouse on Sundays to visit friends or relatives; they always seemed to me to be so lonely, and often they didn't get a good welcome when they arrived.*
>
> *I suppose this was because people did not get a lot of money and there were always a great deal of unemployment in those days so one extra mouth to feed for a day was a great strain.*
>
> *Now I remember that I often thought to myself - 'I hope I never come to that when I grow old'. I think they were very sad days, and it amazes me when I hear people say, 'the good old days'.*

By the time Lydie wrote this article she was at least 77 years old, and she had got her wish, times were better for the elderly if they could get out and about. Clubs for senior citizens had been formed and Lydie together with many other pensioners took full advantage of these clubs. She spent many happy hours making lots of friends, attending concerts and, during the summer months, she had the chance to visit other clubs up and down the country where they would be entertained. Often at the end of the visit they would be given a little gift to remember the day by.

The origins of the Workhouse can be traced to the Poor Law Act of 1388. This Act was brought in to try and correct the balance of labour shortages following the Black Death in 1349, which had claimed the lives of approximately a third of the population. The Act was implemented to restrict the movement of labourers but led to the State becoming responsible for the support of the poor. New Acts were passed over the years to discourage providing relief to anyone who refused to enter a Workhouse. Some authorities hoped to run Workhouses profitably by using the free labour of their inmates, who in general were unskilled. Most were employed to break stones, crush bones for the production of fertilizer, or to pick 'oakum' which was produced from old tarry ropes unravelled and broken down into fibre using a large metal nail known as a 'spike', which might have been where the workhouse's nickname *The Spike* originated.

Life in the Workhouse was intended to be harsh to deter the able-bodied poor and to limit the type of inmate to only the truly destitute, but the institution was often demeaning with families being split up on admittance into different wards for men, women and children. Inmates of the Workhouse did have some advantages though as they were provided with free medical care and education for their children, neither of which was available to the general poor in England living outside Workhouses.

In a report published in 1777 it was noted that the first recorded Workhouse in Bethnal Green was being operated by St Matthew's Church, Bethnal Green which could accommodate up to 400 inmates in premises on the corner of Hare Street and Winchester Street. The Bethnal Green Poor Law Union was formed on 25 March 1836 and 20 Guardians were elected to oversee the running of the workhouse. A new and larger replacement Workhouse was built in 1842 which was able to accommodate up to 1,400 people in several blocks with the inmates segregated into able-bodied in one block, the mentally and physically sick or insane in another block, with a third block for vagrants. This new building was erected on part of Bonner Hill Fields just a short distance from Waterloo Road.

In 1886, *The Lancet Journal* published a damning report on conditions in the Bethnal Green Workhouse drawing particular attention to the lack of adequate conditions in the sick wards. *The Lancet* article however listed Bethnal Green's Workhouse in the top category for the provision of sick-care, 'which can only mean that conditions in the other two categories may have been quite appalling'.

Over time, the Workhouses gradually became the last resort for the elderly, infirm and sick, as Aunt Lydie witnessed. In 1929 fresh legislation was passed and Workhouses were formally abolished in 1930. However, many continued to operate as Public Assistance Institutions. When the National Assistance Act of 1948 was passed, the Poor Law and the Workhouse finally became history and for many who had passed through its portals the end was surely not a moment too soon.

Apart from life in the Workhouse, for those employed in what would later be termed 'sweatshop conditions', life was also harsh. The Board of Trade prepared a report that led to the Trade Boards Act in 1909, this appointed 'Boards' to look into the working conditions of certain types of employment not governed by Trade Union regulations. The main four trades were tailoring, chain manufacture, lace and paper/cardboard box production: all these trades were plied by people working very long hours for a mere pittance. Often the wage could be described as much lower than a 'living' wage. The Boards were an amalgam of representatives both from employers and employees and, to give an even handed approach, a proportion of impartial outsiders. The objective of the Boards was to look into both working conditions and wages, to set guidelines for working conditions and to recommend a minimum wage. Their deliberations were passed on to the Board of Trade whose job it was to implement changes. Slowly attitudes were changing and, for the working man, the change though very gradual would be for the better.

3

Events and History Pre-World War One

Susannah's grandmother, **Annie Taylor,** lived for a while with the Nortons. She is listed in the *1891 Census* as being a lady aged 80 years old of 'independent means'. Life was still, for many inhabitants of Bethnal Green, one of poverty with high unemployment in many parts of the district. In 1911, the National Insurance Act gave limited assistance to those who were too ill to work or unable to find employment. Relief could be claimed in the form of clothing and/or coal coupons, as well as food by applying for small grants to the Poor Law Guardians. The 1908 Budget had included the provision of an 'old age' pension for every elderly person in Great Britain. This was a non-contributory scheme which paid a pension to every person aged 70 years and over the sum of 5 shillings (25p)[4] per week and to married couples a joint pension of 7 shillings and 6 pence (approximately 35p) per week assuming their total income from other sources did not exceed 10 shillings (50p) per week. The Prime Minister, Lloyd George, was blessed thereafter for this magnanimous act, even though he had not been the instigator of this legislation, merely the implementer. This year also saw the Children's Act which was in part designed to protect children in employment.

---

[4] Using inflation, 5 shillings (25p) is a little more than £26.00 in today's values, but measured by the increase in average earnings it is more like a current buying power of £120.

While the family was still residing at 20 Thorold Street, Bethnal Green, their eldest daughter's marriage to James Overy took place on 3 August 1913. Maggie had met James Overy at her brother's 21st birthday party. The two James' were the best of friends, having met at the Oxford House Boys Club, and James Norton was secretly rather pleased when his eldest sister and his friend James married.

Lydie told me many years later that the night her sister Maggie met James stood out in her memory. There had been such happiness in the preparation of the party with family and friends all helping with food, the loan of chairs and other essentials for a large gathering. The house seemed filled with happiness that evening and Lydie recalled her older sister sitting by the window, gazing out at the night sky with a gentle smile on her face, long after the last guests had left the party. Lydie asked her sister why she was sitting there smiling, to which Maggie replied, "I think our brother's friend James is very nice." It was just a few months later that James proposed – so, clearly he had been just as smitten with her.

It was the first Norton family wedding, so great excitement ran through the house. James and Susannah wanted it to be a memorable occasion for the family but especially for their beloved daughter so a lot of love and care was put into it being a very happy day. Many family and friends were invited to the wedding, which took place at St Matthew's Church, Bethnal Green. The parish of Bethnal Green had been created in 1743 and building the church had commenced the same year. Over the years the building has undergone many changes including being rebuilt in 1961 following its destruction in the *Blitz* on 7 September 1940. The vicar who married them was The Reverend Dick Sheppard. Although he was the Vicar of St Martins-in-the Fields, as a good friend of James Overy, he agreed to conduct the wedding service at St Matthew's Church, Bethnal Green.

James Overy held Reverend Dick Sheppard in very high regard. Many family members testified that the mere mention of the Reverend's name would bring forth a glowing tribute from James. I am including a little history of the Reverend as a reminder of his wonderful work in the community, and as a testimony to a man who touched the lives of so many including those in Bethnal Green.

The Reverend Hugh 'Dick' Sheppard was educated at Marlborough College and then at Trinity Hall, Cambridge (1901-1904). He undertook voluntary work in social activity centres run by university people, which were known as 'settlements' for the poor and socially deprived in the East End of London. He became so interested in this that after graduating he began full-time work in one of the best known Settlements – Oxford House, Bethnal Green.

One of Dick Sheppard's main responsibilities was running boys' clubs, and it was here that his popular name 'Dick' was coined, in preference to the formal 'Mr. Sheppard'. He was held in high esteem by all the young men who came to Oxford House because they felt that in spite of his privileged education he could truly understand and identify with them and their needs and aspirations. He also became, for a year, secretary to the Right Reverend Cosmo Lang, Bishop of Stepney. Dick Shepherd then studied for the ministry at Cuddesdon College and was ordained a priest in 1908.

With the onset of the First World War, Dick Sheppard spent some months as chaplain to a military hospital in France. Within a week of arriving, he noted: 'War is more awful than I supposed possible.' Dick identified himself with every dying man and it was noted that he would sit there with the soldier in the last hours of the dying man's life. He felt it might somehow comfort the poor fellow, who was often long past any comfort. He had a breakdown due to overwork in 1915.

After World War One, having witnessed unbelievable suffering inflicted on so many during that conflict, Dick Sheppard become a pacifist and remained one for the rest of his life. He became one of the leaders of the newly emerging English Peace Movement during the 1930s. He famously wrote to *The Times* in protest against a *Victory Ball* to be held in the Royal Albert Hall planned for the evening of Armistice Day:

> *A fancy dress ball on a vast scale as a tribute to the Great Deliverance which followed on the unspeakable agony of 1914-1918 seems to me not so much irreligious as indecent.*

Such a stir was created that the Ball was postponed indefinitely and Dick Sheppard was asked instead to lead a simple service, 'In Memory' at the Hall in the presence of the King, the Prime Minister and other national figures.

In 1924, the British Broadcasting Corporation approached Reverend Sheppard to ask if he would consider becoming their first ever radio chaplain. He saw the potential of this new medium for spreading the Gospel and soon sermons were being broadcast throughout the nation. A charismatic speaker, he soon became famous as the 'Radio Parson'. His radio fame led to opportunities to write columns in popular newspapers on the subject of pacifism and on the recommendation of the Prime Minister, the King made him a Companion of Honour. Shortly afterwards, he became the Dean of Canterbury.

He died on 31 October 1937 of an asthma attack and is buried in the cloisters of Canterbury Cathedral.

A recent photo of the Oxford House 'settlement' building in Bethnal Green. The building faces the present day Weavers Fields.

A later and additional memorial to Sheppard was the naming of one of the first purpose built girls' comprehensive schools in Lambeth (under the auspices of the London County Council – later the Inner London Education Authority in 1955). The school was at its inception well equipped and, like Tulse Hill Boys' School, was seen at the time as in the vanguard of comprehensive education.

Returning to the two Jameses, they had met through their involvement with the Oxford House Boys Club, established in 1884. It was the first university Settlement. The inspiration behind it came from Keble College, Oxford University. The Settlement building was designed as a home for graduates, tutors and those intending to enter the church so that they could learn at first-hand about the problems of disadvantaged areas and provide practical support for the local community.

James Overy's bride-to-be, Maggie, was, in the words of anyone who knew her 'an angel'. She greatly resembled her mother in temperament and was described by contemporaries as having a beautiful wide smile, dark liquid brown eyes, straight dark hair and a beautiful complexion. She had a generous nature as the following story testifies. After their wedding Maggie and James travelled to the coast for a few days' honeymoon. They were booked to stay in a boarding house and duly arrived late that evening but owing to a mix up at the boarding house they ended up staying in different rooms on their wedding night!

With their brief honeymoon over they settled down to married life in a couple of rooms at 20 Thorold Street. James had started his working life as a Druggist's Assistant but, by the time of his marriage he was working for Charrington's the brewery firm as a Drayman (beer was delivered by horse and cart in those days, with the Drayman driving the dray horses to pull the cart).

The dray cart was an open-topped vehicle with high sides which had a ladder or sturdy planks of wood underneath at the back used for rolling the barrels into the cellar. Often children would jump on these planks or ladders for a free ride – until the Drayman spotted them!

Charrington was a major employer in the area at the time. The company had been founded by Robert Westfield in the early 18th century with premises in Bethnal Green but had moved into new premises, Anchor Brewery, in Mile End in 1766, the same year that John Charrington became a partner in the company. Charrington eventually became the second largest brewers in London.

Brewing had been a well-known trade in the area for centuries. Charrington's was not the only employer in this trade at this time other well-known firms were Truman's in Brick Lane and Mann Paulin and Crossman whose premises were in Whitechapel Road.

James and Maggie's first child, a boy, James, was born in May 1914 and was named for his father, but the child sadly died aged three months old from gastric enteritis. Infant mortality was all too frequent an occurrence until well into the 20th Century. The little boy's arrival had been greeted with such joy but sadly he departed life all too soon.

The next pregnancy was to have a much happier outcome when their daughter Margaret Elizabeth Harriet was born on the 30 September 1915. Margaret was born 10 months after the start of World War One (known then as *The Great War* until another took place) but no one who served or loved ones left behind to worry, thought of it as 'Great' other than in the destructiveness it wrought on their lives.

4

World War One:
The Home Front 1914-1919

Although the spark for *The Great War* occurred in 1914, the Imperial Powers of Europe had tried for some years to keep the lid on the simmering pot of international tensions, such as the Balkan Wars of 1912-13, but the alliance system of this period was to prove fateful to the peace of the world. On 26 June 1914, the assassination of the heir apparent to the Austro-Hungarian Empire and his wife was carried out by a Serbian nationalist, in Sarajevo.

Austria declared war on Serbia when Serbia refused Austria's unrealistic demands for compensation. Russia had an alliance with Serbia to mobilise and enter any war on the Serbian side. Germany had an alliance to defend Austria if threatened by Russia. Consequently Russia mobilised as if sleep walking, to be matched by Germany – so all were drawn into war. Meanwhile a military alliance existed for mutual support between France and Russia. Britain had a long standing treaty to defend the neutrality of Belgium, together with France. Ultimatums were ignored and, as Edward Grey remarked – the lights went out across Europe. Germany had a strategic military plan which was designed to avoid the worst dangers of a war with two major powers on two fronts. Based on a plan drawn up by the German General Staff – the Schlieffen Plan – the idea was to knock France out of the war first. France already had a large standing Army and could mobilise more rapidly than Russia, and distances were not so great. Unfortunately the stout and rapid defence put up by the British Expeditionary Force and the slower than planned advance of the German Army turned the plan into a new form of static war and the 'Trench System' was born. A war 'designed' for six months and victory for the Central Powers turned into a bloody four year war of attrition, the deaths of tens of millions and the fall of four Imperial Powers.

So, Britain, and the British Empire, were drawn into the conflict when Germany declared war on France and proceeded to march through Belgium, a neutral country but, by the treaty signed in 1839, Great Britain was forced to honour its promise to aid France in maintaining the neutrality

of Belgium. Britain was also mindful that if French ports fell to German control their loss would threaten Britain's ability to trade with the world. No one could have foreseen the terrible waste of so many lives or the far reaching changes that would come about as a result of the war. All of these events were a broad international backdrop

which affected every hamlet and great city in the country, not the least being Bethnal Green and its people.

On 3 August, a proclamation by King George V, (above) was made public, calling out all "Men of the Royal Naval Reserve, Royal Fleet Reserve and officers and men of the

Royal Naval Volunteer Reserve." This proclamation gave the first serious indication to the British public of the gravity of the situation in Europe and its probable effect on Great Britain. James Norton, as did many a patriot at the start of the war, enlisted as a mariner. He served on various ships including HMS *Wildfire* and HMS *Pembroke*. At that time, Britain was known as *the* world maritime power: its navy was its greatest defence being an island nation. However, a large army was now required for potential operations on the Continent.

On 4 August 1914, Britain formally declared war following the failure of Germany to guarantee Belgium's neutrality. Soon after, the *East London Observer* newspaper began to print details of *The Great War's Preparations and Anticipations*. Motor buses which ran between Blackheath and Bow Road were requisitioned by the War Office to be used as ambulances, while other buses owned by the London General Omnibus Company were commandeered by the Army. Horses were sought and requisitioned in large numbers by Army officers; amongst the businesses that were forced to part with their horses were local breweries – Mann, Crossman & Paulin Ltd; and Charrington & Co. Police and fireman were called upon to sign up as naval reservists leaving many stations inadequately manned.

It was reported in the *East London Observer* at the beginning of August that the 1st London Division's Royal Engineers, whose headquarters were in Victoria Park Square, Bethnal Green, were being mobilised and that their services would be extremely valuable in war as they had always undergone sound training in their particular line. The local public took intense interest in the battalion's movements as they daily awaited the troops' departure. The newspaper went on to report that Colonel Walters was the battalion's commander and he and his men would surely be a credit to the borough.

At the outset of war, many men, including those of the Norton, Overy, Bates and Deeks families had rushed to enlist to serve their country, encouraged by the government's enlistment campaign and in the belief that the war would be over in just 'a few short months'. Young men did not want to 'miss the war'. Apart from the now famous picture of Lord Kitchener directly pointing out of the poster with a caption of *Your country needs you!* Other recruiting posters also called on men to *Fall In – answer now in your country's hour of need* or *Fill up the ranks! Pile up the munitions!* Calling on men to join up, in time, became conscription.

Many young men, everywhere, lied about their age in order to enlist. The local Recruitment Office was situated at 10 Victoria Park Square but as the numbers peaked in August and September 1914 some schools were also used to process the recruits. One such young man was Thomas Polston of Warner Lane, Bethnal Green. He was wounded while on active service in France but returned safely home and lived to see the end of World War Two (he died in 1946). His cousin, William Polston, of Menotti Street, Bethnal Green, was not so lucky though. He served from 16 July 1916 as a private in the 3rd Battalion, London Regiment Royal Fusiliers, until his death on 28 June 1917 aged 23, leaving a young widow. There are many such stories of the young men from Bethnal Green.

Huge numbers of able, professional or skilled artisans had rushed to arms, arguably the cream of the population. The losses in talent were enormous. Gradually the full extent of the horrors of modern warfare seeped into the national conscience and volunteer recruiting slowed. In 1916 the Military Service Act was brought in to ensure that a continual flow of men were drafted into the services. All single men between the ages of 18-41 were then liable for enlistment, by May of that year this included all married men. With the advent of compulsory conscription the only exceptions were those considered to be in 'a reserved occupation'. However, many were exempted from service due to poor health or if they were found to have flat feet!

Conscription brought order to the process by ensuring a steady flow of new men but provided for a sifting out of those in essential work. Conscription, certainly registration, began almost as soon as the Second World War began, based on the lessons learned in 1914-18. On a local level, many lives were to change with the onset of war. It was reported in the local papers in September 1914 that recruiting meetings were often pre-empted with stirring renditions of national songs and anthem played by the band of Doctor Barnardo's Home. Many Music Hall stars performed patriotic songs to aid recruitment, among which was Marie Lloyd, in 1914, with her famous recruiting song:

> *Didn't like you much*
> *Before you joined the army, John,*
> *But I do like you, cockie*
> *Now you've got yer khaki on*

On 26 September 1914 *The Eastern Post* ran an article entitled *War and Unemployment*. The article stated that the war had already had a detrimental effect on employment in Bethnal Green. At the Coroner's Court, Doctor William J Potts, medical superintendent of the Bethnal Green Infirmary was asked by the coroner if there had been any difference since the war in the number of infirmary patients. Dr Potts confirmed there had been a steep rise in patients at the Infirmary of 70-80 extra cases each week. He went on to say that in a majority of cases this was due to poverty. So many of the family breadwinners were now away at the front that those left behind had suffered privation leading to ill-health. He confirmed he had not come across an actual case of starvation but he felt that was due to a greatly increased poor relief being granted. The Coroner agreed there was less money amongst the poorer classes with so many being unemployed. The other side of the coin was also noted, that is to say, that in many instances wives of reservists were having the time of their lives, the husbands had been used to their wives working to provide the extra money they wanted now they could keep this cash for themselves.

As the months turned to years many families were torn apart by the loss of their kinsfolk. East London saw great numbers of their sons and husbands leave home to serve their king and country many of whom by the end of the conflict would lie eternally sleeping in a foreign field or return home mutilated either mentally, physically or both.

During this time, Sylvia Pankhurst, who vehemently opposed the war, was aghast when her mother Emmeline and sister Christabel decided to support the war's conscription drive. She had as far back as 1912 become unhappy and disillusioned with the Suffragette Movement and formed her own organisation in 1914, *The London Federation of Suffragettes*, opening its headquarters in Old Ford Road. When George Lansbury, a supporter of women's rights, decided to stand for election, Sylvia organised a rally in Victoria Park to bring his policy to the public's attention. Sylvia's Federation set up 'cost-price' restaurants to feed the hungry, even dispensing free milk. The Federation also established a toy factory to employ women and a nursery for their children. Sylvia and her team worked tirelessly defending the rights of soldiers' wives and widows with the inception of legal advice centres, continually campaigning to bring the plight of the soldiers' wives and widows to the government's attention. She supported the *International Women's Peace Congress*, held during the war at The Hague, which lost her some of her allies at home.

Parliament at the outset of war realised that Britain could be starved into submission if merchant shipping were intercepted by the German Navy which did indeed attack merchant shipping, particularly in coastal waters. Many tons

War or no war life went on and James Norton Jnr married his girlfriend Harriet Woolcott in 1915, whilst on leave. Before he left for war, he had his photo taken in his mariner's uniform for his mother.

of food were lost to the seabed by enemy action. However the professionals in the Navy were initially against convoys in principle suggesting that the large numbers in a convoy presented a better target to the enemy.

At the outbreak of hostilities the submarine was greatly underrated by the Royal Navy and it took the sinking of three armoured cruisers in the space of an hour on 22 September 1914, by a single small U-boat, with almost 1,500 sailors killed or drowned to bring awareness of the serious threat from undersea attack. But the real danger was to the much slower merchant navy. Astoundingly, protected convoys were only employed in troop movement and it was not until the Germans were sinking merchant ships at a rate which exceeded production that convoys were systematically introduced as late as the summer of 1917 with an immediate halving of U-boat successes. Again, learning from the past, in the Second World War the convoy system was introduced at once.

As time went by, with the losses at sea, any available space was taken for food production. As an island, Britain was dependent on many imports from overseas and so the struggle for supremacy of the seas between German U-boats and British merchant ships escorted by the Royal Navy was a key to survival.

Although the War was fought in mainland Europe, towns in Great Britain were attacked by air, including London. On 31 May 1915, London suffered the first airborne attack in history when the Germans commenced Zeppelin raids. On that day 120 bombs were dropped in an area from Stoke Newington south to Stepney then north to Leytonstone causing 7 fatalities. The raids continued into 1916 by which time London's defences were able to shoot down some of these attackers. The government's recruiting campaign had included posters with the words – *It is better to face the bullets that be killed at home by a bomb.*

On 7 May 1915 the sinking of the *Lusitania* by the U20 cost 1,198 lives. Among the fatalities were 128 Americans, which had an immediate impact on American public opinion and for a time caused the Kaiser to stop his policy of 'unrestricted' attacks on all shipping in British waters. When the news became public locally anger and resentment towards any 'German' locals, often Jewish by the sound of their names, brought immense tension onto the streets. Public opinion swung against these 'foreigners' who by definition of their names were neither patriotic nor loyal to Britain. Crowds gathered outside German Jewish shops – or indeed any establishment with a German sounding name to ransack the premises. The police appeared to be on the side of the resentful crowd taking no action to prevent such unlawful acts.

Sadly, some of the premises were owned by families of German descent whose sons were away fighting in the British forces! However, many Jewish families were technically still German or Russian citizens as they had never been naturalized. That they were 'non-British' citizens bred hostility, in particular towards those of German and even simply Jewish origin, thus leading to anti-Semitism which over the years led to organisations whipping up these feelings for their own purposes as detailed in later chapters.

At the outset of the War, as men enlisted, women were employed to fill the vacancies in a wide variety of employments from van/tram drivers to office clerks, which had until 1914 been regarded as traditionally male employment. During late 1914 and early 1915, Government contracts gave women employment in industries, including ammunition factories that had been expanded to supply troops with uniforms and equipment. In 1915 Phoebe Bates started work in a factory in Gibraltar Walk, Bethnal Green sewing buttons onto military uniforms. A Zeppelin raid took place while Phoebe was at work, one of the bombs dropped very close by the building and the explosion caused chunks of plaster to fall off the walls and ceiling onto the workers below. Phoebe, badly frightened by the experience, ran out of her work place and did not stop running until she reached her dad's premises in Virginia Road. Her dad was furious to find his daughter had been in such danger, rushing outside into the street, he looked skywards, and angrily shook his fist at the departing Zeppelins shouting – "Bastards! Come down and fight like men!"

The London Small Arms Company was based in Old Ford Road, Bethnal Green. It had been founded in 1866 and had a significant role to play during World War One, as it produced components for famous rifles including the Lee Enfield. The factory was near to the canal so parts were easily transported to their other factory based in Enfield, Essex. Even now the rifles produced by this company are greatly sought after by collectors who value the high standard of workmanship that went into producing these iconic British Army infantry weapons. Sadly the factory closed in 1935.

Phoebe's brother, Ted Bates, enlisted in the Royal Engineers on 28 February 1916 as a reservist then on 28 April he was sent to fight in France. He was taken prisoner of war by the Germans on 21 March 1918 in the period later known by the Germans as the 'March Offensive' – an all-out attempt to gain victory before America's manpower arrived on the Western Front in larger numbers.

Elizabeth Norton and Ted Bates had married in 1916; they had set up home together above his father's premises at 113 Virginia Road, Bethnal Green. Ted Bates was originally reported as 'Missing in Action', but eventually it was confirmed that he was a POW: his last place of internment was Pachim, Germany. He recalled years later the treatment meted out: "You would be given rotten food and no shoes. We had to wear rags tied to our feet and our jailers often spat at us." He was not the only member of his family to suffer at this time. His brother Bill, who served in the Royal Field Artillery, was gassed and his brother-in-law, Charles Deeks, was wounded; all three survived the war but like many others they never forgot their experiences.

At home the war permeated everything and there was always concern that German spies may be in the midst.

Slogans were instigated by the War Office as a reminder against careless talk. One of these declared:

A Wise old owl lived in an oak
The more he saw the less he spoke
The less he spoke the more he heard
Soldiers should imitate that wise old bird

James Jnr and his new wife set up home together in the family house in Thorold Street, Bethnal Green – this was meant to be a temporary arrangement while James was on active service but when their son James Edward Norton was born on 29 May 1916, Harriet found her husband's family very supportive in her newly acquired role of mother and so stayed with them. James was not able to see his baby son for several months but what a joyous reunion it must have been for them when he did come home!

When James was on leave, family photos of the proud parents with their son and the whole family were taken to mark the occasion. Sadly, as was the case for countless families, the leave period seemed all too short before James returned to active service.

In 1917 a new airborne threat was aimed at London by the German Military's Gotha bombers. With the realisation that the swift approach of German bombers would leave little time for the civilian population to take cover, the government needed to devise a strategy for air raid warnings. The Police Commissioner in July 1917 announced that police officers would, from then on, wear placards with the words:

Police Notice TAKE COVER

and, when notified of an impending raid, the officers would cycle their beat as quickly as possible to warn civilians of an imminent air raid. A further warning of three 'sound rockets' would be fired in quick succession from the rooftops of London Fire Stations. The ALL CLEAR was also given by the police and bugles would be sounded by Boy Scouts to accompany the written warning. These warning plans would eventually give birth to the siren warning system implemented in World War Two.

Further desperate measures included, in May 1917 before the convoy system eased losses, a Royal Proclamation ordering the well-heeled members of society to abstain from eating food containing wheat as it was a staple food of the poorer classes.

By the autumn of 1917, huge queues formed outside empty butcher and grocer shops. At the beginning of 1918, carefully planned rationing was introduced (another successful procedure, quickly re-instigated in the Second World War). No one was exempt and all were issued with ration cards for meat, sugar and butter. Women and children queued for many hours in all weathers to obtain the family rations – members of the public could also be fined for hoarding food, not that many of the local population of Bethnal Green would have been in a position to hoard.

With the family growing in numbers it was time to find a larger more suitable house and so after some searching in the early part of 1918 they moved into 49 Approach Road. The area around Victoria Park was known as a 'nice' area where people who were in regular employment chose to live. They packed all their belongings and, with the help of family and friends, moved to their new home. During that period working people did not use the services of a removal company. Working class families, even if they were in regular employment, could not afford such luxuries, but instead every available receptacle from boxes to cases would be filled with the families' belongings and transported by hired horse and cart or hand cart or simply be carried to the new home.

The whole family soon settled into their new home in Approach Road. Susannah and James lived in the basement and the rest of the family had their rooms on one of the three floors above. However, the centre of family life was always the kitchen in the basement, where news was exchanged over joint daily domestic chores such as shelling peas or jam making. It was always a welcoming room and the centre of warmth and affection was Susannah who always made time for everyone crossing the threshold.

Shortly after the move, Able Seaman James Norton returned to active service and his wife discovered she was pregnant with their second child. All the family were delighted for her and she joyfully wrote to tell James the good news.

James never saw his little daughter Lydia as his ship went down on 24 January 1918. He was 27 years old.

**The last family photograph
In which AB Norton was present**

The record of his death was finally found by his niece Susie, Lydie's daughter, many years later at the Imperial War Museum, which reads as follows:

**James Henry Norton - Age 27 Able seaman
No 47559 HMS Goliath
North Sea grave reference: 28.**

However HMS *Goliath* was sunk off Galipoli in 1915 so possibly James saw serious action elsewhere because he was killed when serving in British waters. It appears that in 1918 he was a member of the crew of X6, a motorised lighter which, together with lighter X110 were being towed by H M Tug *Desire* when they were intercepted by a German U Boat two and a half miles off Filey. The U-boat sank the tug with gunfire and 'laid bombs' on the two lighters. Sixteen sailors were lost in the action including James, (further details are shown in Appendix 'A' p.268)

The family were devastated when the dreaded brown envelope containing form B10482 arrived. People always believe or hope that tragedy will not strike their own family, somehow they will always be safe. Susannah and James tried hard to dam their grief at the loss of their only son while he was still such a young man with his whole life ahead of him. They knew they needed to be strong for their widowed daughter-in-law, a young mother with a second child due in a few months' time and whose hopes for a bright and loving future with James had been so cruelly snatched away by the futility of war. Harriet was understandably distraught and could not have coped without the exceptional support given by the Norton family. They were one family among so many others who lost a family member during World War One who drew together to help each other through their grief and I tell what family facts I have in order to express the heartache this news bought to so many families.

James' and Harriet's daughter Lydia was born safe and well, she was named for her aunt and grew into a bright little girl, always keen to learn and to try new things. She had a close bond with her older brother James (known as Jimmy in the family). The family had at first been notified that James was 'missing presumed dead', which must have been an agony to live with, especially as the War Office at that time was unable to confirm where his body lay. Susannah never accepted that her son was dead, she always felt he would be found safe and well somewhere. Her granddaughter Lydia told me many years later how she would accompany her grandmother to various war memorials listing those who had died in the Great

War. As Susannah had never been taught to read and write as a child, she used to stand in front of a Memorial, a little lady, proud and erect in her black dress, coat and hat and ask Lydia to read the names out to her. Lydia dutifully did this, but found it such a painful task searching for the name of the father she had never known while her grandmother silently wiped tears from her eyes. As Lydia reached the end of the list her grandmother would say, "There! His name is *not* there, so he must be alive still."

Many churches had plaques in remembrance of those who lost their lives during World War One, and St Matthew's Church, Bethnal Green has a fine wooden version, as illustrated on this page.

During the Whitsun Bank Holiday, 19-20 May 1918, Bethnal Green was again targeted from the air. This raid was the last and largest on London during the War, when 38 Gothas and 3 'Giants' took to the skies from Belgium; 6 Gothas were shot down; another was forced down; 49 civilians were killed and 117 wounded with more than 1,300kgs of explosives dropped. Each bomber had been ordered to target a specific area of London. Bomber number 8 was ordered to East London. Its first target was Poplar, which it bombed just after 11am. Shortly afterwards the bomber began to drop its weapons on Bethnal Green. The Allen & Hanbury Pharmaceutical Works were destroyed along with a row of houses in Corfield Street. During this final raid, 3 people were killed and 17 injured in Bethnal Green.

Until recently, many war dead - both identified and unknown - were laid to rest in the place where they had lost their lives. In northern France and Belgium the large and beautiful World War graveyards are today a testimony to the huge number of lives lost. However, when World War One ended, many relatives of the fallen had hoped that their relatives would be returned to be buried by their families but the decision was taken by the Government not to repatriate the bodies hence the great number of War memorials in many towns and villages listing those who had lived locally but whose remains were never found or who were laid to rest in a foreign field. Soldier's remains are still even now being discovered by Belgian and French farmers. In London on 11 November 1920, King George V unveiled a permanent memorial, *The Cenotaph* (empty tomb), to all those who had sacrificed their lives for their country in the 'Great War'.

Many refugees from Belgium came to Britain, forced to flee the onslaught of the Kaiser's armies, and many made their home in East London, including the father of my step-grandmother, Elizabeth Carter, who appears in later chapters.

By the end of the 'Great War', four of the major imperial powers – German, Russian; Austria-Hungarian and Ottoman had ceased to exist as Empires. The former two lost a great amount of their territory at the end of the war while the latter two were broken up completely which resulted in the central and East European map being redrawn. The League of Nations was formed in the hope of preventing another such conflict. The Treaty of Versailles was drawn up and, by signing the treaty, Germany acknowledged 'all the loss and damage to which the Allied and Associated Governments and their nationals had been subjected as a consequence of the war imposed upon them by the aggression of Germany and her allies'.

This clause was also inserted into the treaties signed by the other members of the Central Powers but later became known to Germans as the 'War Guilt' clause. The treaties also required the defeated powers to pay reparation. The Treaty of Versailles caused enormous bitterness in Germany and later nationalist movements, especially the Nazis, skilfully exploited this. Runaway inflation in the 1920s contributed to the economic collapse of the fragile German democratic government and the payment of reparation was finally suspended in 1931.

These events led to another even more devastating global conflict in 1939 when the grandchildren of the Norton, Overy, Deeks and Bates families would be called upon to fight for their country. Post-1918, the war debt of many countries left weakened economies which would later fall prey to the economic collapse known as 'The Great Depression'.

During and after the Great War, families began to make a small shrine in their garden (if you had a garden) to a lost loved one and Susannah and James erected a little memorial to their son. The memorial was an archway that had been built against a brick wall with a sloping shallow roof; within the archway were shelves and a plaque with his name and unit. Susannah always ensured, except in winter, that there were fresh flowers placed in a vase on the memorial, and in the summer pots of geraniums, her favourite flowers, would fill the shelves in memory of her son James.

Some years later a letter from King George V arrived enclosing what is known as a 'Dead Man's Penny' The 'penny' is a memorial plaque approximately 12.5 cm (5 inches) across. This award and the letter eventually passed to James' daughter Lydia who kindly sent me photos of both.

BUCKINGHAM PALACE.

I join with my grateful people
in sending you this memorial
of a brave life given for others
in the Great War.

George R.I.

5

The Great Influenza Epidemic of 1918

Children's Contemporary Rhyme:

**I had a little bird,
Its name was Enza
I opened the window,
And in-flu-enza**

It is said that as one person dies another is born and although James died a few months before his little baby daughter's arrival, there was another baby born into the

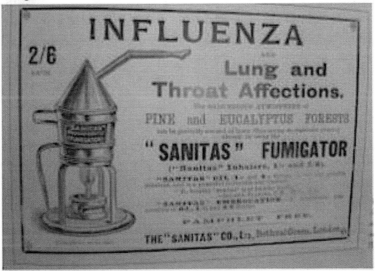

family that year. The new infant was a boy born on 1 November 1918 to James' much loved sister Maggie. The year of 1918, though ending with the Armistice which halted the 'war to end wars' held a much greater threat to all.

1918 was the principal year for the depredations of what was termed the 'Great Influenza Epidemic'. Maggie was one of the victims. In fact the event was a *pandemic* and estimates vary as to the numbers carried away by the outbreak – somewhere between 30-50 million world-wide – or as many dying in a year from an invisible virus as were killed in the recent global war. Thousands of soldiers in demobilisation camps, having survived the war, died of the infection. The civilian population was also ravaged.

The word for influenza was given by the eighteenth century Italians because, with the lack of any other substantial evidence, they decided it must be a product of an astrological influence of the universe, so they named it 'influence' (or as they say in Italian: *influenza*). Most people only suffered this debilitating illness for a week or so but some, such as poor Maggie who had a weak heart, were very ill for many weeks. As many as 10% of those infected, died. It was still some years before the discovery of antibiotics that would be used today to treat the side effects of influenza and more recently protection has come with the use of vaccination. Even now influenza remains a very serious illness, but is better understood.

Unlike most previous annual common outbreaks, the 1918 'Spanish Flu' attacked the young and healthy, rather than children and the older members of the population. There were various 'treatments/apparatus' in the 20s and 30s available, which were optimistically advertised as being the perfect cure. One such company – *The Sanitas Co Limited* was based in Bethnal Green, London.

Maggie's heart condition, coupled with the latter stages of pregnancy, made this illness harder for her to fend off. Her baby was due in late November but, perhaps because of his mother's illness, he decided to make his arrival into this world a few weeks early.

Nearly all births at this time were home deliveries and the women of the family, as was usual, were present at the birth of this little scrap of humanity (my dad). The doctor was duly called as the actual time of the birth drew near. The baby was very small at birth; in fact he only weighed 2 lbs (less than a standard sized bag of sugar). The doctor examined him and then passed him to Maggie's sister Lydie.

The doctor declared, "He is very little and not full term so I don't think he will survive. I will write and sign his birth certificate and prepare his death certificate while I am here. I will not sign the death certificate yet as I will be back to check your sister again later today."

Lydie looked down at her new nephew and felt she had to do what she could for this little baby. Her sister had already lost one son and would be distraught to lose a second. She had no idea how to perform such a miracle but decided that warmth might help and so she wrapped the little baby boy in cotton wool and put him in a box by the open fire to keep him warm. She then turned back to see what help she could give to her sister.

That simple act of instinct may have saved my dad's life and when the doctor returned later that day to check on the mother, to his disbelief, the baby was still alive and looked better than he had at his birth a few hours earlier (shown on next page). Slowly, over the next few weeks, the infant began to thrive and gain weight. Sadly, no one knows what happened to Ted's 'first' death certificate but he often joked that his claim to fame was he had a birth and death certificate written out for him on the same day.

The baby was named Edward James Henry. So, now Granny and Granddad Norton had two grandsons (Jimmy and 'Ted', as my dad was later known) and two granddaughters

(Margaret and Lydia). It took a while for Maggie to recover from the birth and from the Influenza. She never conceived again which was a blessing given that she had a weak heart.

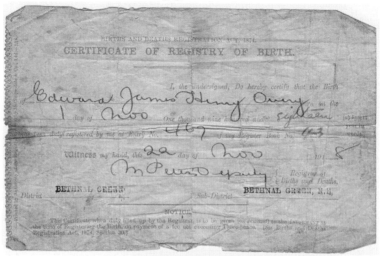

The pandemic was probably spread far and wide in Europe through troop movements during World War One and after the Armistice. It is now thought that the centre of the epidemic was at Etaples in northern France which was a major camp and hospital position. The probability was that, like most Influenza epidemics the start point was in the Far East. In Europe, the constant movement of troops to and from the front made the spread of the disease speedier. The Allied Armies eventually named the epidemic 'Spanish Flu' in the mistaken view that Spain was where the disease originated in Europe – Spain was not a participator in World War One and thus was not subject to wartime censorship, leaving the press to freely report on the spread, new cases, and fatalities – particularly as the King of Spain was himself reported to be very ill with the disease.

6

Annual Events, Special Celebrations and 'Hopping'!

Although life could be harsh at times for all working class families, family gatherings, parties, outings and annual events were a part of most people's lives. No doubt some families were less able or less willing to participate but often this would be due to lack of resources. The following are family memories in the Borough that give a broad idea of how people's lives were drawn together in a way that now seems lost to us but for them brought a richness to their lives. These families were not unique in their ways but by including some of their recollections we may be able to put flesh on the historic bones of life.

Ted Bates' family lived nearby, they were old family friends. In fact, his sister Phoebe had given birth to her first child, also named Phoebe, on 12 November 1918 (it was a productive year for babies). Phoebe Bates had married Charles Deeks the previous year; he was a furniture maker and woodcarver who had a workshop in Virginia Road, Bethnal Green. There were many of these little workshops at that time run by skilled artisans often of Huguenot descent. Charles Deeks was proud of his little daughter and, with an eye to the future, he purchased some walnut wood which he left to season in his workshop (sadly most wood now is unseasoned i.e. not left to dry out naturally and settle to a shape before being cut). When she grew up and met her future husband her father made her, as a wedding gift, a dining table, four chairs and a cupboard from this fine wood. Phoebe was 94 years old when she died and widowed many years but she still had this beautiful gift that her father had lovingly made for her.

A housing boom in the mid to late 19th Century gave rise to the need for large quantities of furniture and many more cabinet and furniture maker businesses were first established at this time.

The Bates, Overy, Deeks and Norton families often called in to each other's houses. Their children, being in each other's company, grew up as if they were all cousins. Families were, until just after World War Two, traditionally very closely knit and because they all lived nearby it was usual for families to take an active part in their children's and grandchildren's daily lives and for the adult children to care for elderly parents. Even so, not all children were welcomed into the world with joy at that time.

To emphasise this, there is a story that Phoebe told me of events one night, not long before she was born. Her parents had spent the evening at the Nortons', no doubt to see the newest arrival, Maggie and James' son little Ted. As they walked home Phoebe, who was near to full-term herself, noticed a little ragged bundle near an archway in the shadows. She and her husband were about to walk on when they heard what sounded like a whimper coming from the depths of the bundle, they went over to check and found a new-born baby. Phoebe, though heavily pregnant, wanted to pick up the baby and cuddle it as she was saddened to think of a tiny little new-born baby being abandoned especially on such a cold, damp night. Charles called the police, who came and took the child – the baby would have eventually been placed in an orphanage if his mother could not be traced. Phoebe and Charles Deeks' daughter (Phoebe) sometimes wondered what happened to the child; she hoped it had a happy life after such a harsh start. Many abandoned children, perhaps crippled, or retarded in some way, or even a child born out of wedlock would be placed in orphanages. There was a church in Bonner Road run by the National Children's Home which became known as *Cripples' Church*, no doubt due to the poor physical condition of the children who sought relief from within its walls.

Phoebe Bates' mother, Mary Ann Bates nee Durrell, had died young and Phoebe took on the role of mother to her younger siblings. She was remembered as an extremely kind and loving lady with a very good nature. One of her younger sisters, Marie, came to her rescue when she found she had been 'persuaded' to take on the weekly washing of the church surplices, as a favour. An angry Marie took the washing back and gave the vicar a strong reprimand for asking in the first place!

Ted and Elizabeth were, in time, blessed with their first child, a boy, born 2 July 1920 and named Albert Edward, (although throughout his life he was known as 'Eddy'). Ted and Elizabeth could often be found visiting the family home at 49 Approach Road. All the family members enjoyed family outings, a favourite being a picnic in Chingford Forest.

Margaret recalled some of these outings and told me that for the children there was always great excitement before one of these Sunday trips. The children would anxiously wait to hear if it would rain. Once Granny had decided, following a studied look at the skies, that the weather would remain fair, they would set off early. All the men would carry the bags of goodies that Granny had baked in anticipation. Large pies, sandwiches and jars of jam would fill the bags but one bag had only a single item in it – the large grey metal family picnic kettle which could hold up to twenty cups of tea. There were no tea bags at that time so a large muslin bag would be filled with the correct amount of loose tea for all the family and this would be put into the kettle once it had been boiled over a fire.

Margaret laughed when telling me of one occasion. Her father must have accidentally knocked his bag against the wall as they left the house. No one noticed, as they walked to Cambridge Heath Station, the trail of plum juice dripping out of the corner of his bag!

The journey on the train would take approximately thirty minutes and by the time they arrived the children were eager to explore, play, climb and run around. While the picnic was unpacked, and to keep the children amused, Margaret's mother would organise a contest to see how many different wild flowers each child could find, offering a prize for the best bunch. The children loved these competitions and put a lot of effort into finding the best and most varied bunch as they knew they would get a special treat – a 'Walls' ice cream – for their efforts.

Ted recalled that if a bottle of cream soda was included in the picnic then a cup filled with cream soda and topped with a scoop of ice-cream would fizz up into delicious foam when it touched the soda, a little bit of heaven to the children. I remember myself being given this treat as a child and agree it was a delight to taste. One outing did end in a soaking though.

Everyone had been ready and eager to set off but clouds started to gather just as they were about to leave. Granny and Granddad Norton looked at the sky and then at each other. Granddad Norton, always an optimist, said they should go anyway. As they reached the forest, the rain clouds opened.

"Probably only a passing shower at most," said a still optimistic Granddad Norton. They all got a soaking that day and Granddad was teased about his weather forecasting skills for a long time afterwards.

Susannah's son-in-law, my granddad James Overy, was a keen gardener and did most of the gardening at Approach Road, keeping both front and back gardens immaculate. He would grow beans and tomatoes for all the family but he also grew flowers, as he knew his mother-in-law and wife were both very fond of flowers. Granny Norton loved the old fashioned marigolds that grew in one patch of the garden and would sometimes pick a bunch to give to a friend or neighbour who needed a little 'cheer' as she called these flowers.

Although there was still a great deal of hardship during the early part of the 20th Century, and after the Great War, there were many annual events that were eagerly anticipated by the locals. Each year the annual Bonfire night, in honour of Guy Fawkes' capture and execution, would take place, though this event was banned during both world wars. Just like other children in Bethnal Green, the boys – Jimmy, Ted, Eddy and later Artie – would make a Guy from old clothes they begged from Granny Norton, and they would stuff their 'Guy' effigy with any old rags they could find, paint a face on the head, then beg for an old hat (no self-respecting Guy could be seen without one!). It was quite commonplace at that time, to take the Guy out to sit with them and ask for a 'penny for the guy' from passing pedestrians. Any resulting collection would be put towards fireworks, which all the family would enjoy on 5 November, being the only night fireworks were set off (unlike modern times) and bonfires were lit with the poor old Guy being sacrificed atop the bonfire. Within the edges of the bonfire would be placed potatoes to roast and these would be eaten to warm everyone.

One year the children in the Bates family almost suffered a fatality. They were out collecting 'pennies for the Guy' when one young boy's scarf slipped down and became entangled in the wheel of the cart, and as his siblings pushed the cart forward the scarf began to tighten around his neck!

Christmas was another annual event enjoyed by all. Even those on low incomes would celebrate in whatever way they could. The Norton Christmases were a magical time for the children and memories of these Christmases were passed on to me, giving a wonderful insight into people's lives and some of the ways people celebrated during the period. The planning and preparation each year commenced many weeks before the event in order to make it as memorable as possible for all the family. There were no shops advertising Christmas items for sale before the start of December but what excitement when the first few seasonal items appeared!

Gradually the market stalls with their gas flares, to allow shoppers to see their wares in the gloom of winter, became more and more festive. The hustle and bustle gradually increased as Christmas drew near as did the cries of the stallholders inviting shoppers to buy their goods. Right up to Christmas Eve, shops, stalls and shoppers were out to buy or sell all the last minute items. A good deal of good-humoured haggling, particularly in the final hour or so, would take place with every housewife keen to stretch the housekeeping as far as possible but for those families on very meagre income it could be very hard if not impossible to provide even tiny gifts for the children whose fathers could only find casual work. Pickpockets and thieves looked forward to the festive season as they always have done and probably always will.

For many weeks beforehand the children were encouraged and helped to make little gifts. Maggie Norton was very good at creativity and would show the children how to make little pin cushions, pen wipers, hair tidies etc. All the presents would then be carefully wrapped and labelled, then children would be given the task of making the endless paper-chain decorations to be festooned around the parlour.

You always knew it was getting near to Christmas in the Norton household when the special pair of dark pink curtains came out of their box and were hung in the parlour window. They were only ever seen at Christmas and afterwards would be carefully taken down, shaken, wrapped and stored again for the next Christmas.

Susannah Norton would have been busy for weeks before in the kitchen with festive food preparations such as mince pies and of course the Christmas puddings. The puddings would be put into the large 'Copper' and boiled for hours in the hot steamy water. This process ensured they would keep for months, though they rarely survived Christmas.

On Christmas Eve, the adults would put Christmas presents in pillow cases, one pillow case for each child. Once the children were fast asleep (or appeared so) the adults would creep into the girls' and boys' bedrooms and place their pillowcase at the foot of their bed. Ted recalled there would be such excitement when you saw your pillowcase – all misshapen with various strange shaped packages – and lots of gasps and giggles as they scrambled into the depths to find and open each gift but no matter what else they might find in their 'sack' there would always be an orange, an apple and a small bag of nuts. Many poor children would have been grateful for just the fruit and nuts. There were always pre-Christmas threats to the children against their being 'naughty' – Father Christmas would not bring them any gifts other than a lump of coal if they were naughty, which kept them well-behaved, briefly.

On Christmas Day just before midday, all the family would gather downstairs in Granny and Granddad Norton's kitchen for Christmas dinner after which they would slowly stagger into the front parlour, stomachs full of food. The older members of the family would settle down for a snooze, if they were lucky enough, while the children were happily playing. The families were aware of how lucky they were and how many of the people in the district would go hungry at this time of year. Granny Norton always ensured that any clothes or shoes the children had outgrown were parcelled up and taken to the local church and as many pennies as could be spared would be donated to help those in need.

After tea the family would entertain the children with old family games such as – 'Have you met Lord Nelson?' This game involved all the children being sent out of the room. One of the adults would sit on a wooden chair and put on a jacket but they would only place one arm in a sleeve – the other sleeve would have a wooden broom handle in it! In their other hand would be half a nice juicy orange! Each child would take their turn to be blindfolded and led into the room where 'Lord Nelson' sat. They would be invited to touch Lord Nelson's good arm and then his 'bad' arm which usually drew a sympathetic sigh from the girls. The child would then be invited to touch his good eye and then the 'bad' eye! Oh the squeals when their finger was plunged into the unseen juicy orange. In spite of the fright all the children loved the game, even when they again participated in this game at future Christmases – the juicy orange 'eye' still drew shrieks.

There was another game that I recall, known as the 'Norton Family Game'. My parents still played this at my childhood parties. All the children would leave the room with two adults. A third adult – the 'mind-reader' – would stay in the room sitting on a big chair with a little chair next to it for a child to sit on. Outside in the hall each child would be asked by one of the adults what he or she would like as a present for their birthday or Christmas, then the adult would lead the child into the room and tell them to sit on the chair. The 'mind-reader' would be asked if they would like to guess what the child would like. The adult who had led the child in of course knew what the child wanted, so began asking the 'mind-reader': "Do you think that the child would like a jigsaw puzzle?"

The 'mind-reader' would pretend to consider this and then say, "No!" and continue to say no to each suggestion until the adult suggested a toy with 'wheels'. The 'mind-reader' would know that the very next item suggested would be exactly what the child wanted. All the children would be very impressed and delighted with the bag of sweeties they were given and would sit happily munching these as each child took their turn. The children were quite in awe of such a clever person who could read their minds. I am sure other families played similar games but I just knew it as *our* family game.

New Year's Eve was always spent at Aunt Elizabeth's and Uncle Ted's. They bought a Christmas tree each year which would have on it a few extra little gifts for New Year's Eve for each member of the family. Aunt Elizabeth and Uncle Ted would organise a raffle too, with a fairy doll for a girl and a suitable small toy for a boy. There were often a few tears from the losers but they soon dried their eyes with the promise of special Christmas sweet treats to come later.

One year, young Margaret found some silver leaves in a drawer at home and asked her mum (Maggie) if she could wear them. Margaret, like her dad, enjoyed dressing up. Maggie smiled down at her little daughter and helped drape the silver leaves in her hair. Margaret remembered walking to her aunt and uncle's home with her head in the clouds – she felt quite grand. Aunt Elizabeth smiled when she saw her little niece's head adorned with silver leaves and asked if she had hoped to be the fairy on the top of the tree. They all laughed at this.

Aunt Elizabeth was very kind and full of fun. She and her brother-in-law James Overy would often dress up at these New Year's Eve parties. On one occasion James wore a ballet dress with a wreath of flowers in his hair while still wearing his boots as he danced around the room with a giggling Aunt Elizabeth. Until the advent of television most families would entertain themselves, their family and friends a great deal.

Everyone was expected to do a 'turn' at these parties – dancing, singing or perhaps reciting. There would be many a groan after the 'entertainment' and much good natured teasing about two left feet or singing in a different note to the key played by the pianist! Aunt Lottie's friend, Kit, who for a time lodged with the Norton family, was frequently the pianist and apparently a very good one too.

There would be strange little prizes for the best in each group such as a broken umbrella or an old hammer – nothing useful, especially to a child, but that did not deter them from their willingness to participate. All the children enjoyed dressing up, except Jimmy who was a little shy compared to the rest of the children. He always wore a Father Christmas mask to hide his embarrassment when it was his turn to perform.

To give a theatrical setting the parlour door would be taken off its hinges and a special pair of curtains would be hung in its place. As each performer took their turn the curtains would be theatrically opened and the pianist would play a fanfare as the 'entertainer' was revealed. Everyone had their own little set performance and over the years you would get to know each performer's party piece. This meant that there was a lot of 'joining in' at times with much fun and laughter if the performer changed the routine slightly to catch the audience out.

Holidays and day-trips to the seaside were a favourite with both adults and children, but an outing one Bank Holiday to Ramsgate landed poor young Ted in trouble. Ted had been given a small sailing boat which he insisted on taking to the seaside. He had tied a long piece of string to the boat and kept putting it down on the floor and pulling it along.

The family arrived at Liverpool Street Station where there were large crowds of people milling around all intent on travelling that day. The children were told to keep close to the family. Margaret was rather intimidated by so many people tightly packed around her; she clung to her mother's coat as she was frightened she might get lost in the crowd. As the family edged slowly through the ticket barrier, Ted somehow managed to wrap the string on his little boat around the Ticket Collector's feet and in the ensuing melee his new sailor's hat was knocked off and disappeared onto the train tracks. Ted was not popular with the family for a while, but they all had a good day out in spite of this mishap.

The Norton family holidays were usually taken in Yarmouth or Ramsgate. For the children the journey to the seaside would be filled with excitement to start with but, as children have always done, they would get bored with how long it took to get there. Upon arrival, lodgings would need to be located. One particular year the guest house had an invasion of mice! Maggie was absolutely terrified of mice and could not sleep the first night for fear of a mouse popping out and squeaking at her. Suffice to say, the next day they went off to find fresh lodgings.

Families would take rides on the 'Brakes to Pegwell Bay. These were open-topped buses which were drawn by a pair of horses. The illustration is thought to be c. late 1920s.

Many holiday makers would all go for a daily stroll along the 'Prom' (Promenade) to 'take the sea air' as James called it. Ted and Margaret didn't remember the salty smell of the sea air, but rather the smell of fried fish shops and stalls selling fresh wet fish and the small dishes of cockles or whelks with little bottles of vinegar for the customers to sprinkle on their shellfish purchases. Even if the weather was chilly and wet, they would still wrap up in warm clothes and stroll out.

A visit to Ramsgate was Margaret's and Ted's favourite as the train station was right on the sea front, almost on the sands. Once they alighted from the train, there would be men with donkeys and carts waiting to transport you and your luggage to your holiday lodgings.

The children loved to play on the sands and to swim, or in Margaret's, Ted's and Jimmy's case, pretend to swim with one leg on the seabed, (now, how many children have done this?). At noon they would be taken, reluctantly, up the long slope for the midday meal. Usually the lodging would only include breakfast so the family would stroll around looking at the many café menu boards with the day's offerings and prices; there would be many comparisons by the adults of both the menus and prices before the day's choice was decided upon.

A trip on a type of horse-drawn bus, called a 'brake' was a highlight of the time, when a family was visiting Ramsgate. Pegwell Bay was within easy reach and was an exciting change of scene. A hill lay between the two resorts. Half way up the hill the brake would stop to allow for a change of horses. Then, once at the top, the view of Pegwell Bay would be laid out before them. There was a little public house on the cliffs above the Bay where the adults would quench their thirst. Behind the pub were some beautiful public gardens where the children would happily play until it was time for the return journey to Ramsgate.

The public gardens at Pegwell Bay were spacious enough to have a bandstand. Some evenings a pianist would entertain the holiday makers. The bandstand was decorated with little fairy lights, which were illuminated at dusk and made it seem all the more magical to the children.

Although the pub was high up on the cliffs, there was a footpath from the pub that led down to a little rocky beach far below. The children were forbidden to go down the footpath in the evenings as it was gathering dusk but they loved to sit on top of the cliff and watch the flickering lights over the railings and to see people appearing to be getting smaller and smaller as they descended the path.

It was not only the Nortons who enjoyed Ramsgate so

An outing to Ramsgate. On the left is Susie as a little girl with her mother. The young boy at the left in the front of the photo is Eddy and the two girls behind Eddy are Lydia Norton and Phoebe Bates. The young lad with the long legs is Ted (my dad). Jimmy (Lydia's brother) is standing at the back with Phoebe Bates Snr in front, and next to her is her son Vicky. The other two boys are Artie (Eddy's brother) and Leonard (Lottie's son). Lottie is at the front of the photo and the little boy and his mother next to my dad were friends of Lottie.

much. Ramsgate was a favourite seaside resort with many families from the East End, even if just for a long weekend or a day trip. Ramsgate was and still is a lovely seaside town with a small bustling harbour. Margaret and Ted both recalled a little hut on the harbour. Inside the hut it was dark and in the centre stood a large round table with a map showing the views from the hut that could be seen through the periscope. They would ask their dad to go and stand on the slope above the sea and wave at his children. What excitement when they were able to view him waving at them through the periscope.

During the 1920-1930s, it was normally the women and children who had the longest time away on holiday, the men not having much paid holiday. Usually the whole family would depart for the seaside and at the end of the weekend the men folk would return home to go to work and then re-join the family the following weekend often staying for the second week

Of course, although the Norton family had holidays as all the menfolk were in regular paid employment, not all families were as lucky as they were. Many children in that era would have grown up never seeing the seaside or even the countryside.

There was one 'holiday' that many East End families took each year which was to go 'hop picking' in Kent. Hops had been grown in Kent for centuries as they were and still are a key ingredient in beer production. Each year, farmers would write to families and invite them back to go hop-picking at the end of August.

**Maggie and James with their two children Margaret and Ted
holidaying in Margate. C.1928.**

The families would pack up their belongings including necessary items such as candles, lamps, water jugs, pots and pans into maybe a vacant pram.

The families would walk to London Bridge Station and catch the 'Hopper's Specials' that were run overnight through the county of Kent stopping at virtually every station en route. Because they travelled at night, the fares were cheap but the families were packed in so tightly that children often had to sit in the luggage racks. Frequently to avoid paying the fare of all the children, a child would be 'encouraged' to tell the ticket collector on arrival that mum had his or her ticket and was following behind! The farmer would meet the families at the station with a cart to transport the luggage and the young and old to the farm – the more able-bodied would walk behind. It usually took about four or five weeks for all the hops to be harvested.

During harvest time the families would be provided with very basic accommodation on farms in one storey buildings known as 'Hop Huts' which were approximately 9 square meters in floor space – made of wood or corrugated tin. They were very basic huts with no proper amenities but the visitors did not mind and were happy to cook their meals each evening over camp fires – the farmer provided bundles of faggots (small tree branches) for the fire. It was hard, low paid, back-breaking work. The more you picked the more you were paid, so all the family would be enlisted to earn as much as possible during these few weeks. Year after year, families would return to the same farm they had worked on in previous years. Over time, friendships were formed with the locals who looked forward to the cheerful cockneys' arrival.

Occasionally, families that could afford to, would book a 'Mystery Tour'. The vehicle often used at that time for transporting groups of people would be a *Charabanc*. These were the forerunners of coaches which became a very popular form of transport. These early vehicles were open topped with a soft hood for inclement weather. The word *charabanc* is French and comes from three French words *char a banc* meaning a 'cart with benches'. At first these vehicles were horse drawn but gradually, as motorised vehicles became more popular, the *charabanc's* design was also updated to incorporate an engine and hard-topped hoods evolving from the soft-topped earlier versions, so that by the 1940s they would be more recognizable as a coach similar to those still in use today.

The Nortons loved these mystery tours. Occasionally the tour would take the family to the Lavender Fields in Kent, where they would stop for a cream tea before the return trip. Often on these outings, someone would start to sing and within a short space of time, many of the passengers being in a happy holiday mood would join in. James Overy loved to sing and would sing loudly with great gusto – although Maggie, his wife, a quiet shy lady, would tug at his sleeve and try to 'shoosh' him, but that never deterred him.

By the 1960s, and the advent of almost all households having their own car, the popularity of the 'Mystery Tour' faded away.

7

Victoria Park and Barmy Park

Closer to home there was a place of recreation which still exists and is well used to this day. Victoria Park has for over 170 years been a wonderful and important oasis for local people

Approach Road is, from the outside, little changed since the Nortons lived there and the mature rows of graceful plane trees on either side of the road are still present. The road remained the 'approach' to one of the main gates of the Park.

A recent photo of the entrance to the park from Approach Road. The gate is 'Bonner Gate' after Bishop Bonner, the last lord of the manor of Stepney, whose lands known as Bonner Fields, became part of the park.

Victoria Park was the first public park to be built in London specifically for the local people. The Act of Parliament passed in 1841 made it the first planned public park not only in the

The Boating Lake

Country but indeed the first in the world, which was intended to meet the needs of the surrounding communities. It was built to give the people of that part of London some open space to hopefully help improve their health in what was a very overcrowded and poor part of London. It was officially opened in 1845 although it had been in unofficial use since 1843. In April 1873, Queen Victoria visited the Park that she had been so instrumental in establishing which had been named in her honour.

Victoria Park, known locally as 'Vicky Park', was soon renowned for its annual horticultural displays. Descriptions of its wonderful planting arrangements were often included in the gardening press. Any plants left over, once the annual beds were planted each year, were given away to local people.

The Chinese Pagoda

The park has, over the years, been the focal point for many famous meetings such as the Charterist demonstrations in 1848 and various suffragette rallies. One of the most infamous gatherings was the Fascist meeting in Victoria Park Square led by Oswald Mosley that took place in July 1936 and which eventually culminated in the famous Battle of Cable Street on the 4 October that year.

The park is bordered on one side by the Regents Park Canal.

Victoria Park remains a beautiful oasis in Bethnal Green, with its elegant mature tree lined walks and picturesque boating, still as popular as in Victorian times and, following the demolition of the original, a rebuilt and recently refurbished Chinese Pagoda with benches nearby for locals to sit and enjoy each other's company in convivial surroundings. Joyce Devey recalled how before their marriage Vic Deeks would often take her out in a boat on the lake in the summer.

Victoria Park Lido was opened in May 1936, much to the delight of all those that frequented the Park. It had a shingle 'beach', diving boards and chutes, and a huge pool (200 ft by 90 ft). At first, admission was free three days a week (five days for children). Sadly, Victoria Park Lido, like so many others, has since been demolished. Before the Lido was built the local people had to travel to Hackney Swimming Baths. Aunt Lydie was always keen to take the children and try to teach them to swim and would make the journey to Hackney with them as often as possible. Aunt Lydie and Lydia, her niece, loved to be in water and were quite fearless as they delighted in this aquatic sport. The rest of the children happily went along on these trips, especially once the Victoria Park Lido opened but did not become proper swimmers. They enjoyed just splashing around a lot more!

Ted and Margaret had many fond memories of time spent in 'Vicky Park' with their cousins and friends. During the school holidays the park would be full of children playing, with vendors selling toffee apples and ice cream to those who had the pennies to pay for these treats

Frequently entire families would go to the Park for a picnic lunch. Sometimes, after lunch, they would wander around the well-tended rose gardens and lakes, with little ones toddling along and often a baby in the pram.

People from all walks of life came to Vicky Park; you would regularly see the nannies with their charges walking in the Park, reflecting various contemporary domestic lifestyles. Family tradition has it that occasionally, on their return from the park, the nannies with children would knock on Susannah's front door to ask if they or the children could go to the toilet. Susannah, at first, used to let them in, but gradually word got out that the lady at 49 was very obliging and so the numbers making this request increased. Granny

Norton decided, at this point, that she would have to be firm and say 'no' from then on.

Susannah Norton would always help someone if she could. An example of her kindness was when she noticed a young woman bringing a little crippled boy in a wheelchair to attend the school opposite. The mother would leave the child at school and take the wheelchair back to her home, returning at the end of the school day to collect the little boy. Susannah offered to store the wheelchair each day for the mother to save her pushing the heavy chair back and forth twice a day.

Many locals were of a generous nature in offering help, but

at the other end of the social scale could be found the 'urchins' from the poorer part of the district. Having become 'streetwise' from years of poverty and neglect, many of these children exuded a tough exterior with 'an every child for himself' outlook, but with little kindness in their lives and a lack of proper clothing for nourishing food, the softest character could turn a little aggressive.

Entering the park from Approach Road the first unusual Park feature is a pair of stone 'dogs' on pedestals, one on each side of the main path. These are part of the *Bow Heritage Trail* and are known as 'The Dogs of Alcibiades'. These statues were presented to the Park in 1912. I remember, years later, Aunt Lydie speaking of these and the stories that they – as children do – told each other – each capping the next salacious tale with further embellishments on their view of the legend.

The actual history is a little obscure but Alcibiades was a Greek who docked the tail of a contemporary dog – hence the howling stance.

There is a fine and elaborate fountain in the Park.

This feature's construction was paid for by Angela Burdett-Coutts. Her attention was drawn to the lack of fresh clean water for the local inhabitants so she decided to undertake the provision of a drinking fountain in Victoria Park.

H. A. Derbyshire designed the fountain in a Gothic Italian style. The materials used to build it were Sicilian marble, Cornish granite and Caen limestone. When it was built it 1862, it was seen as an important step forward in preventing water-borne diseases such as cholera. Though today it is no longer in use as a fountain, it is a striking monument in the landscape of the park.

There is also a small park next to Bethnal Green underground station; this area was the nucleus of Bethnal Green in much earlier times. On one side of the Green, on the present day site of the Library, stood Bethnal House, known locally as Kirby Castle. The building was not a castle but a

A recent picture of the pathway leading to Bethnal Green Library. Barmy Park is still a pleasant place to sit and reflect on your surroundings.

fine Elizabethan house. After a long and varied ownership Bethnal House was converted to a women's mental hospital. A further building was constructed as a hospital for mentally ill men. Having both these hospitals in such a small area led the locals to rename this open space – they christened it 'Barmy Park!'

In spite of this rather colloquial epithet the space remains a delightful oasis, albeit close to a busy junction. The 'park' is well used by the locals, particularly in the summer. Those who went before will rest easy that their vision of public use for perpetuity was justified.

8

Everyday Family Living and Housing Associations

Many families were clothed in good serviceable attire often made by the women of the family. The other source of clothing for children was known as hand-me-downs. Many working class adults would make do and mend, making their own or buying second-hand clothes from markets such as Petticoat Lane, one of the many famous markets in the area.

Maggie Norton was a skilled needlewoman, which was just as well with a growing family to clothe. She loved to make her daughter pretty gingham dresses as well as practical items such as aprons and warm winter coats. Like her mother, Susannah, she adored making herself hats. During this time no self-respecting woman would go out without a hat but Susannah and her daughters made hats with feathers or flowers or both. The hat in the picture on page 67 was probably made by Maggie, who also had a talent for making fancy dress clothes out of simply anything that was going spare.

Susannah Norton loved feathers and would create wonderful hats with graceful plumes that waved regally in the breeze as she walked along. They were very ornate long after the fashion for such opulent headgear had passed, which gave rise to her grandchildren being teased about 'Grandma's hats'.

Ted was a typical child of his times. When he was about three years old, his mother made him a warm smart coat for the winter. Many hours were spent on this task and when it was at last finished to her satisfaction, she dressed Ted in the coat and took him down to show her mother how nice he looked in the finished coat. Ted duly trotted down the stairs with his mother but Granny Norton was not in the kitchen. Maggie went into the garden to find her mother, leaving her little son to wait in the kitchen. The table was laid for tea and Ted could not resist looking to see if there were any of his favourites on the table, and yes there was: a new pot of blackcurrant jam. No one would know – would have been his thinking – if he just *tried* a little of Granny's home-made jam. He quickly dipped two fingers into the jar but before he could put them in his mouth, his mother and Granny Norton returned. Hastily he put his jammy hand into his new coat pocket. Granny Norton proudly looked at her grandson with a loving smile and told him he looked a very smart little boy, but her praise soon turned to despair when she and Maggie saw the blackcurrant jam stain on the pocket of his new coat. Maggie had to make another coat pocket and coat lining; blackcurrant jam is not that easy to remove from some materials.

Families and friends (like the Norton, Deeks, Bates and Overy families) used to be part of each other's daily lives, frequently speaking to each other on all subjects as families often lived close by making it easy to just drop in. This was an age before telephones became a household item unless you were of the 'upper' classes. One such friendship was between Maggie and her sister-in-law Jenny.

Both Margaret and Ted have spoken to me of this close and special friendship between the sisters-in-law. They had many shared interests and enjoyed each other's company immensely (this sort of close friendship was not unusual for those living in the area) – families were very closely knit especially in East London. Jenny married James' brother Walter and they had two young sons.

Jenny and Walter lived in a flat in Bethnal Green near to the railway. Margaret and Ted said they always enjoyed a visit to their aunt, uncle and cousins as they could always play in the enclosed drying space above the flats. Line upon line of tenants' washing was a regular sight but it did not deter the children from playing hide and seek among the washing lines. Aunt Jenny was a very easy going woman who took life in her stride no matter what and a few children playing among the washing was not going to matter to her so long as they were safe and happy. At other times they would play in their aunt and uncle's sitting room with the miniature railway set, with the track laid under chairs and around table legs. The railway set belonged to Margaret and Ted's cousin Walter who was always happy to share his train set with his cousins and friends.

Uncle Walter was one of 10 children, born and raised in Bethnal Green. He was a butcher by trade. He worked hard and over time managed to buy several shops; once the businesses were doing well enough he decided it was time to move his family to a nice house of their own in Highams Park near to Epping Forest. Many people from the East End would be impressed if someone they knew was able to move to Highams Park because you had definitely 'arrived' if you could do that. Jenny and Walter still saw all their friends and families as often as they could, either visiting others or inviting people to their new house although the longer journey meant they did not see each other as often as they had before.

Most families from Bethnal Green were unable to achieve such success and spent their lives in frequently damp terraced houses with an outside toilet and no bathroom, or if they were lucky enough they may have had the chance to rent a small tenement flat such as those in Guinness Buildings, Columbia Road. These flats were built by *The Guinness Trust* which had been formed in 1890 by Sir Edward Guinness to provide housing for the inner city poor. There were other housing enterprises set up to alleviate the living conditions of the poor in East London. Two such enterprises were the *Four Percent Industrial Dwellings Company* founded in 1886 and the *East End Dwellings Company* founded in 1882. During the 1870s when slum clearance commenced, both of these companies sought to provide basic sanitary accommodation. Every flat was built with two rooms with shared facilities of toilet and kitchen with another flat. Such was the shortage of housing that many flat dwellers also took in a 'lodger' to supplement the family income.

The Four Percent Dwellings Company decided to employ superintendents to ensure that the flats did not degenerate into slum dwellings. The superintendent was given strict guidelines and powers to choose not only the tenants but to evict those he felt did not meet the required standards, regardless of why the tenants failed to achieve these standards. The 'Rules' for the tenants were pasted onto walls for all to see and were draconian – examples of these rules being: 'No clothes or unsightly objects are to be exposed to view'; 'all rooms are to be kept exceptionally clean'.

The tenants were also required, on a weekly rota, to wash and whiten the passages and stairs of the block they lived in. Failure to do this task to the required standard would result in the superintendent tracking down the person responsible that week and demanding they repeat the chore. Rents had to be paid weekly with one week in advance and failure to comply for whatever reason often led to eviction. One such eviction in 1912 was of a Russian widow and her three small children who fell into arrears. The widow had pawned everything she owned of value but the superintendent refused to listen to her pleas and pressed ahead with the eviction, witnessed by a young girl:

The bailiffs threw everything that was left over the landing, later on the family quietly returned and moved in with us for a few days but when the superintendent found out he told my mother we could be thrown out too!

Other tenants, angered by the harsh rules, took it in turns to let the family stay with them. Eventually an anonymous benefactor paid the rent on behalf of the widow so she and her children could return to their former home. Fortunately, this case in particular led to a relaxing of the harshness of the rules from then on.

Once Walter moved his family to Highams Park, they decided they needed some transport to undertake the long journey back to visit their families so Walter purchased a motor bike and side-car, then decided to pay his brother and family a 'surprise' visit. The bike drew up with a roar and Margaret and Ted could see it was their uncle astride this machine wearing a biker's leather flying helmet and goggles. Aunt Jenny and the boys clambered out of the side-car, grinning from ear to ear. By now all the Norton family who were at home that day came out to see Walter's family and to admire their mode of transport. Walter offered to take Margaret for a ride on the bike. She was a little nervous but rather pleased that she had been chosen for the honour of a ride. Margaret got on the pillion of the bike and off they went along Approach Road towards Vicky Park then through the gates into the Park itself. Uncle Walter increased the speed as he drove around the Park but Margaret was not so keen once the bike's speed quickened and clung onto her uncle as if her life depended upon it. Before she knew it, they had arrived safely back home where Margaret gladly dismounted the bike and walked a little unsteadily into the house to catch her breath and comb her long wind-tousled hair. Maggie must have been nervous to see her daughter ride off as a pillion passenger and equally glad to see her safely home, even if she was a little shaken and white faced from the experience.

Susannah took an interest in all aspects of her grandchildren's lives and liked to be as supportive as possible in their activities. Lydia had become keen on sporting activities and knew that her grandmother would always make time to come and watch her and cheer her on if she was taking part in the 'School Sports Day'. Lydia liked her grandmother taking an interest but, being often teased about Granny's penchant for wearing those old fashioned feathery hats, decided, one year that rather than offend or hurt Granny Norton's feelings she would avoid telling Gran the date of the School Sports Day and persuaded her cousins not to mention it either.

All went well until the day before Sports Day. Lydia rushed home with her cousins from school, eager to have tea and go out to play. Granny smiled at Lydia and said she had some good news for her. Granny told her she had by chance met the school's headmistress that morning and they had stopped for a few minutes to speak. During their conversation the head mistress mentioned that Sports Day was the very next day and asked Granny if she was going to attend as usual. Granny, proudly telling Lydia of her chance meeting that morning added that the headmistress had kindly offered her a seat next to her on the stand so that she could have a good view of all the events. Granny thoroughly enjoyed the day but Lydia, although triumphant in her sporting events, had to take a fresh round of the annual teasing about Granny's hats from her school chums.

**Family photograph early 1920s.   (back row) Margaret, Jimmy
and Lydia with (front row) Eddie and Ted.**

Young Ted's mischievousness as a child meant the blame for any misdemeanour was usually laid at his feet first but, in fairness, rarely was he blameless. One such incident took place on a late summer evening. Dusk was approaching and the children all knew that they would be called in from play very soon. At that time, the occupants of Approach Road came from many walks of society, from manual workers to professional people, their station in life would often be indicated by the little floor covering each household displayed on their front doorstep. Ted came up with the bright idea of swapping all the mats: the school teacher's Axminster rug was placed outside the hardware shop owner's door, his old worn piece of lino was placed outside the grocer's door, etc. All the children had such fun swapping the mats around; then they all went home to await the outcome. One boy was sent in to let his mother know that someone had taken their front door mat! Soon all the neighbours were outside, oil lamps in hand as it was by now dusk, looking for their doormats. Ted was not allowed out to play in the street or the park for a few days as punishment.

Margaret remembers another occasion, during a winter's evening, when the children were equally mischievous. The children slept in two rooms on the top floor of the house. They had been put to bed as usual in their respective bedrooms. Once they had been wished goodnight, they would be left more or less to go to sleep and not be expected to be seen or heard until the morning.

It had snowed all day and outside lay a crisp white layer of snow, not slushy as it could be sometimes, but perfect for making snowballs. This particular night, at the public school opposite the house, there was a function taking place. The children looked down on the scene out of the window. The lamps leading up the steps to the entrance were all lit and cast pools of soft glowing light to guide the attendees into the building. The children had gathered in one room to watch the people arrive. The girls were in awe of the ladies' outfits but the boys could see an opportunity for a little bit of fun that evening. They crept down the stairs and outside the house to fill, quickly and quietly, a couple of containers with snow. Then they returned to the top floor where they made snowballs and pelted the unsuspecting guests as they arrived. The people arriving looked around them puzzled as the wintry missiles landed but could not see where the snowballs had come from. This was one escapade that went undiscovered by the family's adults.

Although the children all got into various scrapes, they could always expect to be disciplined by the family once any naughtiness was discovered. The children were never smacked for being naughty but the verbal reprimand would be a long and detailed one so that they did not forget it. Sometimes the boys would be made to sit on a chair in the front first floor bay window for a time. When this happened, their friends would see and tease them as they knew they had been caught in some misdemeanour. Ted recalled the times he would be required to 'sit' in the window looking out, wishing the time away so he could go back out into the street to play with his cousins and friends. He also remembered that at these times, he would promise himself he would not be mischievous again but, like all children, their memory fails the good intention.

Another escapade surrounded Ted's 'fringe' which had grown rather long. He kept saying to his sister it was getting in his eyes so she offered to cut his fringe for him. Young Margaret thought she was being really helpful with her offer and Ted was delighted to accept. He sat on a chair with a towel draped over him while Margaret fetched her mother's sewing scissors and a comb. She stood for a few moments in front of Ted staring intently at the offending fringe before starting to cut across in a 'straight' line from one side of the fringe to the other, but when she stood back to check her work the fringe appeared to be shorter one side.

"Not to worry," said Ted, "give it another go." So Margaret tried to cut from the other side of the fringe. Alas, still the fringe was not straight – just a lot shorter! Two more attempts at trying to get the fringe straight left Margaret in tears as she could see that the fringe was by then just a tuft. Suddenly, the two of them heard their mother call them down for tea. They froze to the spot for a moment. Ted stood in front of the mirror to see his 'new look' fringe, Margaret was really worried. Ted was matter of fact about it and told Margaret not to cry. "After all," he said, "it will grow again." He told his sister he would cover his fringe with his hand so no one would notice.

All went well as the two of them sidled quietly into the room. Their father was reading the paper, so noticed nothing at first, their mother was busy laying the table also unaware.

Ted sat down with his hand covering the offending fringe. Margaret sat nervously next to him. "Elbows off the table!" said their father, as he folded and put aside his newspaper. Ted dutifully removed his elbow but kept his hand over his fringe until his father gently but firmly took his hand away to see what was wrong.

James and Maggie were astonished to see the little tuft, where once a fine fringe had been – but realised it was an accident of sorts. The children were told not to do anything like that again and they never did, as children, but Sheila, Margaret's daughter, remembers her mother cutting her fringe crooked when she was a nine-year old child – it seems Margaret never did fine tune the art of cutting a fringe straight.

Speaking of hair, one thing that James Overy loved was to come home from work and sit in his favourite high backed wooden chair and ask young Ted to comb his hair for him. James always found this so relaxing, almost as if young Ted was combing out the cares of the world from his head.

As the children grew, the adults would take it in turns to get all the children ready for bed each night. The children would be called from their play and told to tidy their belongings away before saying 'good night' to all the family. The adults would then supervise the older children and help the younger ones with undressing and washing. Depending on which two adults were in charge would dictate the mood of this nightly activity with varying degrees of giggling and trying to avoid too much soap – especially if you were a boy – lots of soap around the neck was anathema to a boy!

Many years later the enthusiasm and fond memories of times past became very evident to me when Lydia sent me a photo of Approach Road which Susie (I will come to Susie later in the book) made into a Christmas card. Lydie sent me a little note explaining who lived on each floor, and the verse Susie wrote in her card to her cousin that year – see next page.

All the children would have daily chores to do, as part of life for them. They would never argue with their elders, but just get on with the allotted tasks. There was often a certain amount of good humoured teasing among the children if one got a necessary but nonetheless unpleasant chore – cleaning the grates once you were considered old enough or 'black leading' the kitchen range. Short cuts were not allowed – inevitably, a sharp eyed adult would notice and the youngster would be told to do it all over again with the adult watching over.

Suzie's Christmas Card and Lydia's note

49 Approach Road where the family lived from 1918 until bombed out in 1941

But sometimes a misinterpreted word from an adult, and adults being absent could lead to... a memorable moment.

Lydie called the children in for tea and asked Susie to lock the garden side gate before coming in as there had been several incidents recently of theft from nearby gardens.

"What do they do?" Susie asked with a serious face.

"They might steal things."

"What?"

"Pots – things we leave about."

"Toys?" asked Susie.

Lydie nodded gravely, "Just hurry up and come back in quickly."

Having taken in this threat, Susie ran out into the garden to carry out the exciting task. Just as she was approaching the gate, she saw it swing slowly open. She concluded - the warning fresh in her mind – that someone was coming into the garden to steal her toys. She grabbed her brother's cricket bat, left lying where they had been playing, and swung it with all her might at the head that appeared around the edge of the gate.

Lydie was blissfully unaware that her daughter had decided to take such bold action against an intruder. Suddenly, Lydie heard her young daughter give a bloodcurdling scream. Lydie ran outside into the garden and found a young Romany girl lying prone, bump on her head rising even as Lydie looked. Thankfully, the girl recovered consciousness almost at once. The child appeared to be only suffering from a large bruised bump on her forehead. Lydie helped the young girl to her feet, brushed the dirt off her dress then took her inside the house where Lydie applied salve to the bump on the child's head. Lydie felt sorry for the child, for when she looked at her more closely, she could see that the child's clothes had seen much better days and that her feet were bare. The child was just a little smaller than Susie so Lydie, having given the child a drink and some food to eat, left her to see which clothes Susie had outgrown could be passed on to this child. Lydie managed to make up a parcel of clothes and gave these to the child to take home to her mother. The child looked very pleased with the unexpected gift and trotted off. Lydie sighed with relief as the little girl disappeared from sight, then sat down with Susie to explain that cricket bats could really hurt someone so they were only to be used to hit a ball.

The following day the child returned with a scrawled note from her mother. Expecting some kind of threat Lydie opened the note with a touch of trepidation which disappeared at once as she read:

Got any more clothes missus?

When the younger children were old enough to attend school, one by one, their older cousins or siblings would be given the responsibility of taking and bringing home the younger ones. The local headmistress was firm but fair with her pupils and gave immense encouragement to each child to learn and to realise their full potential. Times were hard but an education gave a start in life and potentially helped all the pupils earn their living in whatever trade they chose to follow. The children of the Norton family were fortunate to have parents in regular full-time work and so went to school well clothed and fed each day although this did not mean the family were affluent, far from it.

Many children in the area were from families where the breadwinner was either out of work for periods of time or could only get casual labour work. These men would form queues at factory gates or walk to the docks to try to seek work each day. Often, passers-by would see these sad-faced men waiting anxiously at the gates for the foreman to appear and make his daily selection. At the sight of him, the men would jostle for what they considered a prime position in the hopes of being one of the chosen few.

Many of these men would spend some of their wages in the local pub, alcohol being a means of mentally escaping the grinding weight of poverty for a few hours, but leaving even less money to provide for their families. The children of these families would have an inadequate diet, even attending school with bare feet and threadbare clothing often passed down many times from one sibling to another. In these homes, several siblings would sleep in one bed because of cramped living conditions – perhaps there was some advantage in winter, through shared warmth. In really cold weather, coats would be piled on top of the children for want of extra blankets.

Often the mothers would take in washing to bring in a few extra pennies and the children would be expected to help with what was at that time a very hard living. Perhaps this was another reason why the Nortons tried to ensure the children got a good education to help prevent them falling into a poverty trap in the future. All the Nortons were hard working people who were keen to ensure that they did not get into debt and were able to provide adequately for their families. They appreciated that they were lucky to have regular employment, unlike many of the residents in surrounding areas.

Granny Norton would have been particularly pleased that all the children could read and write well. It must have been hard for her: a lady who, family members testify, was a bright and quick witted woman but denied the chance to acquire these skills. She never bemoaned her lost opportunity and was glad others were able to have a better foundation than she ever had.

9

Shops, Street Vendors and Markets – Early 20th Century

The area in and around **Approach Road** had a variety of shops and trades that would have been common place anywhere in the 1920-1940s. There was a popular public house – *The Approach Tavern*. Whereas streets are mainly filled with the hum of motorised vehicles nowadays, in the early part of the 20th Century the street sounds were of a different and wider variety: the clatter of horses' hooves; the sound of the street vendor with his or her verbal enticement to buy; a sense of everything being local, and within walking distance; the rumble of handcarts as they were pushed along the streets, their metal wheels grinding over the cobbled thoroughfares; hand bells being rung to alert you to the rag and

The Approach Tavern **in the late 1920s.**
(see p182 for modern image)

bone man on his rounds – all provided a background entirely different compared with the latter end of the 20th Century. Shopping tended to be done on a daily basis.

Always the streets would also carry the sounds of children playing games – such as hopscotch, cricket and skipping or feverishly played games of marbles on the pavements, or flicking colourful cigarette cards at a wall. Children could be heard singing, running and laughing together. Almost everyone walked to and from destinations, often stopping from time to time to pass the time of day with an acquaintance. The motorised vehicles that mainly used the main roads included trams running on metal tracks embedded in the road – pedestrians needing to taking care not to catch a heel or a cyclists had to be wary of getting a tyre stuck in the tracks – so the folk-lore ran.

At the time the family lived there, the first of *The Approach Tavern* proprietors were Mr. and Mrs. Brooks. Mr. Brooks was a short, pale, tubby man but his wife was very tall. She always wore a black velvet ribbon around her dark hair. They were not a happy couple, continuously arguing about everything and anything. Locals always knew when they were quarrelling because Mrs. Brooks would sit down in the saloon bar and play the piano – something nice and noisy; she would keep her foot firmly pressed down on the 'loud' pedal to increase the volume still further. Frequently she would sing along to the music too. The children could not resist peeking through the letterbox when Mrs. Brooks started to play, until Margaret and young Ted's father caught them and no doubt gave them a suitable reprimand!

The Brooks had one child – a daughter, Lily – who was the image of her father. A pale, withdrawn child she was often being chastised by the teachers at school for not having her hair tied back as stipulated in the school rules. Lily had pretty light brown hair which fell in curls around her shoulders.

Once, Lily was called out to the front of the hall during Morning Assembly and the head teacher tied her hair back in public with a piece of string.

The next couple to take over the Approach Tavern was Jack and Blanche King. They completely changed the interior of the pub and placed tables and chairs outside for customers to use in fine weather. It became a popular venue with people coming to visit from miles around. Often people who had travelled to Vicky Park would call in there on their way to and from the park.

There was nearby a shop which sold cat meat (there was no specialist food for cats or dogs at that time) and the outlet also did a reasonable trade in second-hand comics. The Norton grandchildren were lucky as Granddad Norton worked in Fleet Street; he often arrived home with new comics for the children – hot off the press!

Once the children had read these comics, they would take them to this little shop to trade for other comics. The shop was often a good meeting place for the local children all milling around the boxes of used comics, eager fingers delving in to find a comic they had not read and the triumphant arm raised high when the treasure was found.

The children would be given pennies to buy the family cat some meat and they would watch in as the proprietor thinly slice the meat, then children went home to tease the cats with these special feline delights.

Beside this shop was a little barbers shop that cut ladies', children's and gents' hair; but the children would have to sit quietly and wait until the barber had served all his adult customers first – adults would leave a tip whereas children didn't, hence the wait.

Next in the parade of shops was an Italian café. The aroma of freshly made coffee would tempt passers-by to perhaps enter and order a cup. As further aids to increasing profits, you could also buy fruit and bottles of lemonade. The bottles were made of glass which would have a marble in the top of the neck of the bottle; you would have to press down firmly on the marble to pour the lemonade out. The proprietor would sell 'specky' fruit, and often a halfpenny worth of 'specky' fruit, once the damaged part had been cut away, would delight a child. Nothing was wasted by either the shop traders or the housewife.

Another example of making full use of every particle of food for sale was the cake crumbs on sale from the baker. You could buy a halfpenny worth of stale cake crumbs and many children would happily devour these.

"What about wedding cake crumbs?" Ted's dad sometimes teasingly asked the children when they returned home with their bag of cake crumbs, "You should ask for wedding cake crumbs, full of dried fruit they are."

On the other side of the Italian café was a little haberdashery shop. The lady who owned the shop was small and neat just like her shop. She sold reels of cottons, ribbons, baby clothes and lace. There was a chair by the counter for a customer to sit while waiting to be served. The proprietress was quite old with grey hair piled up on her head in a bun. She always wore high necked blouses with a little black ribbon around her waist from which her scissors would be suspended. Her shop window was always neatly arranged with assorted baby clothes and other haberdashery items to tempt any passing trade.

At the other end of Approach Road was a small group of shops some of which fascinated the local children. The cobbler's shop was a great attraction and the children would sometimes gather to watch the cobbler at his work. He was a well-built man with large work-worn hands, cobbling had been his trade for many years so he was able to work speedily on the footwear he was repairing. The children loved to watch him gather a handful of boot nails then push them halfway into his mouth, after which he would then daintily pluck one nail at a time from his mouth, and expertly position it over the sole or heel he was repairing before hammering it home in the blink of an eye.

Next door to the cobblers was *Bennett's the Chemist*. The chemist himself was a tall man. He lived above his shop with his wife and two children, a boy and a girl. The family were of German descent. The girl was a bully and therefore unpopular with the local children, she also bullied her younger brother and her mother and any of the local children who were unfortunate enough to cross her path.

A little laundry shop stood the other side of the chemist. Margaret would take her dad's stiff collars there to be laundered and starched each week.

The last shop in this parade was the dairy which was run by a Mrs. Humphries. She had neat grey hair that was always piled high on her head. The inside of the shop was entirely white: walls, woodwork and ceiling with a scrubbed counter and a spotlessly clean tiled floor. The counter had a hinged lid at one end which Mrs. Humphries would raise to come out from behind the counter. On the counter stood a large white crock (ceramic pot) and all around the edges of this crock would be differently sized ladles. Customers would take along their own vessel for filling with milk and state the amount of milk they wished to buy. Mrs. Humphries would then select the appropriate ladle and plunge it into the churn of milk. Out the ladle would come, filled to the brim with frothy fresh creamy milk that she would then pour into the customer's container. There were many of these little dairy shops in this part of London at that time. Often the proprietors were Welsh or of Welsh descent, having left their homes to seek employment when none could be found in their homeland. One such dairy in Bethnal Green is *Jones The Dairy* on Ezra Street, Columbia Road. It had begun life at the beginning of the 19th Century as a small family run dairy but over time it evolved into a thriving quality grocers shop.

Sometimes one of the children would be sent to buy milk from Mrs. Humphries; however, usually the Nortons had their milk delivered to their door. Sterilised milk was very popular as it would keep fresh if unopened longer than ordinary milk. There were no modern conveniences such as fridges to keep food, especially milk, cool and fresh. Often a house would have a covered area outside the back door with a little shelf on which stood a 'safe'. The safe was a cupboard consisting of a wooden rectangular frame with a solid wood base and back. The sides, front and top of the cupboard frames would be filled in with a very fine strong mesh which would allow cool air to flow in and around the food being stored this way. While this worked most of the time for storing perishables for short periods, the downside of course was the effect in hot weather.

The children's favourite shop was next in the row – the sweet shop. This was a small shop full of wonder for any child as it was packed full of exciting confectionery to please the palette of any youngster. The shop was owned by Miss Rosa, a tall dignified lady beloved by all the children. Some of the confectionery delights sold in this shop are no longer made but among those remembered by Margaret and Ted were: tiger nuts, stick-jaw (which lived up to its name), coconut ice, peppermint creams and gob stoppers (a real favourite of Ted's).

As he described to me: "Oh the joy of anticipation as you watched Miss Rosa carefully weigh out your choice and put it into a little poke (a poke was a cone shaped twist of paper), which she would then fold down at the top before handing it over in exchange for pocket money pennies. Needless to say, the poke top was soon opened and the look of delight on the children's faces as they walked home sucking their beloved sweets was a sight to behold."

After a while, another sweet shop opened around the corner to Approach Road. The proprietor was of an entrepreneurial nature with his rather forward thinking sales strategy. He would offer the children a 'lucky dip' for the princely sum of ½ d (Almost 1/500th of the present pound[5]). Once you had paid your money you could choose an envelope from a box. Inside each envelope was a note with the 'prize'. It would either be sweets to the value of ¼d (a farthing) or, if you were really lucky, 4d or 8d worth of sweeties – you were very popular if you got one of these prizes. No wonder the shop was always crowded with children.

Not all of a child's pocket money would be spent on sweets. The Norton children, like many others of the period, if they were lucky enough to be given pocket money, would also be encouraged to save some of their pocket money for treats. One such treat would be to hire a bike.

The man who hired the bikes ran his business from a little shed. Youngsters would pay 6d (in pounds, shillings and pence - £ s d - *d* stands for denarii, hence, here 6d - sixpence) to hire a bike. They were old fashioned bikes but this did not deter the children from the thrill of riding full tilt along the road to the park with cousins and friends, the wind streaming past their face and hair flying in every direction.

---

[5] There were 240 pennies in a pound. 480 half pennies and 960 farthings. A 5p piece today was called a shilling (12d) so there were 20 of these to the pound. There were two shilling pieces (10 to the pound - 10p today – also termed a 'florin') and half crowns, 2/6 (two and sixpence, 8 to the pound and worth 12.5p in today's money). Foreign visitors were rightly confused, until saved by decimalisation on 15 February 1971! Kids of the time grasped the complications from their early years since they were often dealing with the smaller amounts.

There was a wealth of mobile street vendors during this period. The only remnant of street vendors that you see rarely in modern times is the 'Romany' selling sprigs of 'lucky' heather, ice cream sellers in their tuneful vans, the milkman with his electric float and a variety of static stalls at street markets often only held once a week in many towns.

Often little girls could be seen selling matches (hence the famous children's story of the 'Match Girl' I remember reading as a child) or young boys selling bootlaces in the streets. In the winter months the *Hot Chestnut Man* was a welcome sight with hot coals sizzling on the brazier used for cooking the chestnuts. The colder the day the greater the profits he would make. Another seasonal trader were the French farmers mainly from Northern Brittany; they were nicknamed *Onion Johnnies* presumably because John (Jean) was a popular name in France. They would arrive late July after the harvest and could be seen cycling in the streets selling strings of onions, hanging in great plaits from handlebars and every other part of their bikes.

There were other trades too, such as the coalman with his horse and cart filled with sacks of coal in his delivering of customers' orders and the knife grinder with his hand cart. There was a pedal attached to a grinder via a belt, the man would hold the blunt implement to the grinder and using one foot to pump up and down turn the grinding wheel. Rag and bone men were a frequent sight around the streets and they would buy any old rags (for paper production) or bones (for glue production). They would tour the streets pushing a handcart or driving a horse-drawn flatbed cart. They would often trade a cut of salt from a large block in exchange for scrap and old clothes. The *Muffin Man* with his tray of muffins on a strap around his neck and a hand bell which he rang to let customers know he was on his rounds and the *Paraffin Oil Man* to mention but a few of the many and diverse trades then current, most now lost.

A curious side-product of the horse traffic were the droppings from the animals. People with gardens and allotments would go into the streets and collect the 'manure' to help their personal harvests – boys and men with bucket and shovel picking the droppings up were a common sight. The street vendors were split into groups. If all you had was a tray or suitcase to sell your wares from, then you were classed as a 'pedlar' but if you had a handcart or horse drawn cart you were known as a 'hawker'. However, trades people who sold fruit and vegetables from either were always known as 'costermongers' whereas traders who had shop premises were 'green grocers' to distinguish them from 'grocers' who sold just about anything for household use. One person could be seen on the streets twice daily and that was the gas-lamp lighter. He would walk the streets with a long pole which had a hook at the top of it. At dusk he could be seen on his rounds, pulling the latch down on the lamp to allow the gas to flow and light the streets with its soft glow, then at first light he would return to pull the other latch down to cut the flow almost but not quite off, just enough the leave the mantle lit although you would not see the dimmed light in daylight hours. Decades went by before simple clock mechanisms were built into the lamps so causing that particular work occupation to cease to exist. Many of these trades local to Approach Road, described by the family, could be found in roads in and around Bethnal Green. It is worth mentioning here that there are several famous markets in Bethnal Green, many of which have been in existence for centuries.

Petticoat Lane Market, situated in Middlesex Street, was recognised as a market until 1936, but there is a lengthy history of there being a market on this site for many years before and it may well be the oldest surviving market in Great Britain. It was probably named thus as its principal trade had been ladies' undergarments. The story goes that they would steal your petticoat at one end of the market and sell it back to you at the other end! As the years went by the diversification of goods for sale meant that no longer was the market exclusively for the sale of women's undergarments. I remember as a child being fascinated by all the colourful stalls and listening to the tempting sales pitches. I clearly remember the sets of crockery for sale. The trader would, as you watched, pile a full dinner set onto one large plate then toss the set into the air, deftly catching all as it fell.

Old Spitalfields Market (Spitalfields borders west Bethnal Green and many citizens moved from Spitalfields to Bethnal Green in the 19th and 20th Centuries) was a fruit and vegetable market until 1991. There had been a market on the site since 1638 when Charles I gave a licence for 'flesh, fowl and roots' to be sold on 'Spittle Fields'. The market has undergone changes in its long history and today is a popular crafts and fashion market. Columbia Market was established in 1869 by Angela Burdett-Coutts as a covered food market with 400 stalls. There were plans for a railway line to deliver fresh fish to the market but this was never built - traders preferred selling outdoors. The building resembled a cathedral and in keeping with its appearance the bells in the Clock Tower would peal out a hymn every 15 minutes. The costermongers did not appreciate Baroness Burdett-Coutts' attempt to improve their morals and so returned to the back-street stalls. Incidentally, the name 'costermonger' is believed to have originated from the 'Costard', a medieval apple. The market was later used as warehouses and small workshops and was originally a Saturday only' trading place but an Act of Parliament

moved the trading day from Saturday to Sunday to comply with the religious needs of *Jewish* traders. The change in trading day also gave traders on other local markets the opportunity to sell their leftover stock. Flowers and birds were very much a part of the lives of Huguenot immigrant families so gradually the predominant trade became cut flowers with a pub *The Birdcage* at the end of the market giving a reminder of the caged birds that had been for sale here, decades before.

Stalls on Columbia Road Market selling a wide variety of cut flowers, bulbs and plants can still be visited each Sunday as the recent photograph on the previous page testifies.

Brick Lane Market is across to the east of Commercial Street and has always been favoured by people keen to snap up a bargain from a diverse range of goods. It has, over the years, changed the ethnic variety of goods for sale as immigrants have moved out of the area only to be replaced by other nationalities seeking to build a home here. One of Brick Lane Market's famous traders was a Jack Cohen who took on a stall in the market just after World War One to sell fish paste and golden syrup. From this small beginning the household name of Tesco owes its origins.

10

Family Memories from the 1920-1930s

As we grow older, the confidence and ability to learn and adapt to new things can diminish. Sometimes, there can be a fear of the unknown though and one thing that always made poor Granny Norton nervous was the radio, or as it was more commonly known: *the wireless*. In 1922 regular wireless broadcasts for entertainment began in this country from the Marconi Research Centre. The first publicly owned radios were sold as 'crystal sets' in about 1925; these sets were powered by an acid-filled battery. My dad, Ted, recalled how the boys would be sent in turn to a shop to get the battery charged and told to be very careful not to spill the acid out of the battery. Granny Norton was not keen on this new invention, in fact, I know she was a little nervous of a box that could speak to you, understandably so if you think about it.

Post World War One, many young women widowed during the war began to gradually pick up their lives again. Lydia Norton had and in 1924 she met and married her second husband. She moved out of Approach Road and eventually had two children through this second marriage. However, Lydia was not a strong woman and found it very hard at times to look after her four children. Jimmy and Lydia Norton (the children from her first marriage) could often be found at their old home and seemed to miss living there. One day when they called round to see their grandparents, sharp eyed Granny noticed that young Lydia had a nasty cut on her knee. Granny Norton was very concerned and did what she could to clean and dress the wound but after a few days it had not healed. Granny took Lydia to see a doctor, for which she had to pay a fee, and he treated the knee giving Granny Norton instructions for ongoing care.

After a while it was agreed between the Nortons and their daughter-in-law that Jimmy and Lydia should live with their grandparents in Approach Road, which led to the Nortons legally adopting them. The children remained in contact with their mother and half-brothers but were very happy to be back in their old familiar family home.

**Granddad and Granny Norton on an outing with their daughter
Lydie, granddaughter Lydia and grandson Jimmy.**

And so to another happy family event: Charlotte (James and Susannah's youngest daughter) was to wed Leonard Goodwin. The year was 1925. Maggie and Lydie were ten and seven years old respectively and very excited as they were to be Charlotte's bridesmaids.

The girls were so excited as they had pretty new dresses for the occasion and, as a special treat, were to be allowed to stay up later so that they could hear the jazz band at the wedding reception. As the day drew near the girls, especially young Lydia, became euphoric.

The day dawned bright and sunny and, as was the custom, a small crowd of friends and acquaintances gathered outside the house to wish the bride well as she left for the Church. Lydia was ready long before everyone else and, full of excitement, ran down the steps to show her beautiful bridesmaid outfit to her friends. In her haste to descend the steps poor Lydie stumbled and fell cutting her knee but apart from that and her pride being a little dented she was not too badly hurt. However, as she walked stiff legged up the aisle behind the bride, Lydia clutched the veil so hard she almost tore it from Charlotte's head.

After the wedding ceremony, family and friends returned home for the wedding reception. Some of Charlotte's workplace friends had been invited and, to little Margaret's surprise, one of these ladies had a long black cigarette holder. Charlotte had asked permission from her parents for any of her friends to smoke on this special occasion. Many of Charlotte's friends were very modern young ladies. They had their hair styled in the latest fashion, which was known as the 'Eton crop', a short straight hair style often with a fringe.

1926 was a mixed year for the Nortons, their families and friends. First the joy of another addition to the family when Elizabeth and Ted where blessed with a second son, Arthur, known to all as Artie. Another grandchild also made his arrival that year when Charlotte and Leonard had a baby boy who was named Leonard for his father.

This was also a tense time, for the General Strike took place from midnight on 3 May through to 12 May. In the previous year, a General Strike had been planned in support of miners who were being asked by the coalmine owners to take a pay cut and work longer hours but at the last minute the government had granted a nine-month subsidy to the owners and set up a commission to look into the matter in order to avert a countrywide strike. The Commission duly reported back in 1926 approving the original wage cuts so the subsidy paid to the mining industry by the government ceased. The East End, being a predominately working class area, had for years had sympathetic leanings towards the 'workers both in this country and abroad', e.g. during the Russian Revolution of 1917. The unions closed ranks around the miners, organising marches in support with branch banners parading the slogan – *Not a penny off the pay, not a second on the day.* When talks between the Unions and the mine-owners broke down, a strike was called by the Trades Union Congress to support the mine-workers who had been 'locked out' by the mine-owners when they refused to work for less.

Gradually all coal extraction from the mines ceased. Up until the last few decades of the 20th Century the country was heavily reliant upon coal extraction for many areas of the economy including heavy industry and domestic heating. On 20 April, King George V proclaimed a 'State of Emergency' and plans were drawn up and put into action to ensure vital services and industries continued if a strike went ahead. The East End, populated with many sympathisers, was prepared to stand up for their fellow workers. A nervous few days ensued as the Army was strategically placed around the area in order to keep essential supplies flowing from the docks.

This was a serious situation and Margaret recalled how the children were told not to go down to Vicky Park because the Army had, as a precautionary measure, set up camp in the Park in case they were needed to take over essential jobs from strikers or to quell any riots.

Row upon row of white tents could be seen through and over the park railings. However, there were large numbers of volunteer strike breakers who came forward to offer their services for essential and emergency duties and this left the Army, camped out in the Park with little to do other than keep the peace by simply being there.

Margaret remembered being quite frightened as events unfolded during that time; she was scared there would be another war, a real enough fear if you are only 10 years old. She, like the other children of the family, had overheard the adult family members from time to time relive memories of the First World War amongst themselves. Children growing up at that time were able to run and play in the roads and streets near their homes as there was very little traffic to be wary of, so to be kept close to home until the General Strike was over made the children quite apprehensive.

The General Strike was called off when, just over a week old, and in-spite of all the rhetoric and militancy of the unions and the Communist Party, the miners had to return to work for longer hours and less pay. Bethnal Green and the rest of the East End still harboured a sense of perceived injustice and during the next decade the rise of Fascism would once again fan the embers of unrest within the community.

11

Illness, Death and Domestic Life
in the 1920-30s

In **Bethnal Green from time to time** there were outbreaks of serious illnesses and from 27 September to 30 December 1924, 88 cases of typhoid were notified; 81 of these were proven to be genuine cases, 11 of which were to become fatalities.

The first case on 27 September was linked to a milk supplier, Messrs, Chapman, The Oval, Bethnal Green. But further cases were notified over the next few days with some of the later cases being linked to another milk supplier Messrs. Morgan Evans, 34b Green Street, Bethnal Green. Investigations revealed that the proprietor and manager, Mr Morgan Evans, was ill in bed (he lived with his family above the shop premises). Mr Evans' doctor was attending him having diagnosed a condition similar to influenza.

The authorities and the doctor discussed Mr Evans condition and it was decided to transfer him to the London Hospital on 2 October where, on the following day, a confirmed diagnosis of typhoid was pronounced. Once several cases of typhoid fever with a common link to Messrs. Evans were identified, the hunt for the actual source began with an exhaustive examination of the shop premises, cow shed and cows but the results were inconclusive. The Public Health Committee distributed posters advising residents of Bethnal Green to boil all milk until further notice. The outbreak was serious enough and of long enough duration for a *Special Report on an Outbreak of Typhoid Fever in the Borough of Bethnal Green* to be published early in 1925 as no other borough at that time had reported any typhoid outbreaks.

Many families would, in this period, have known the frailty of life and the consequences of the death of a family member. Following the arrival of Jimmy and Lydie within a short time, two more cousins joined the family to live at 49 Approach Road, again, for a sad reason. Elizabeth was by all accounts a lovely gentle lady, perhaps like her sister Maggie she could be described as being too good for this world. She had a succession of colds and coughs that left her unable to fight off further infections. Eventually she was admitted to hospital, where in 1928 aged 32 she died.

Her boys were very young and Ted, their father, had to go to work to provide for his family, so Granny and Granddad Norton now had four grandchildren to care for. Their daughters Lydie and Charlotte (Lottie) were wonderfully supportive and a great comfort to them. Often when a death in a family left small children without a parent at this time, it would be the extended family that would help raise the orphans.

Susannah and James took the additional work in their stride but it must have been hard for them. Luckily Granddad Norton and their sons-in-law were all in regular work (there was no State welfare, if you fell upon hard times, other than Poor Relief).

The shopping alone for so many mouths would have been a large enough task in itself but Granny Norton took it in her stride, coping with the additional responsibility to feed and clothe all the family members more than adequately. Margaret recalled often meeting Granny

Norton at one of the shops to help her carry home some of the heavy bags of shopping. As time went by though, some of the groceries were delivered to the house to help her. There was also additional cooking, cleaning and, above all, an awful lot of washing each week. The boys would be sent to the sawmill where an uncle worked and he would give the boys barrow loads of offcuts, misshapen pieces of wood – but to the children some of these shapes would look like wonderful playthings. They would have loved to have been allowed to keep a few of them to play with but knew that all the wood was needed.

On wash days, the boys would put the offcuts on the 'Copper' fire to heat the water. The fire would need to be fed regularly and stoked to heat the water with many more of these off-cuts until all the clothes had been washed. There was no such luxury as an automatic washing machine and no inbuilt brighteners in the washing powders during the 1920s and 30s. It would take Granny Norton all day to clear all the dirty washing using products such as 'blue' to get the washing really white and 'starch' to give the clothes and linens a crisp finish. She would have pummelled the bed sheets and other whites in a tub with a heavy wooden Dolly, and at some point all the individual items would have had water squeezed from them by running them through a Mangle, steering the garments with one hand as she turned the rollers with the other hand. This was heavy work, which often called for two people when it came to the 'mangling of the sheets'.

Then, after the laundry was dried, came the ironing. Granny had a set of 'flat irons' – these were cast-iron and heated on the cooking range and each one used in turn to press and smooth the cloth. Once the flat iron cooled, it was put back over the heat. You would wet your forefinger (or spit on the iron) and just lightly touch the bottom of the iron – if it hissed as the wetness on your finger met the heat of the iron, then it was hot enough to use, if the moisture 'exploded' the iron was too hot. This was a skill much admired by the youngsters.

As mentioned earlier, many poor families would take in washing; a family of one of Margaret's friends did so to supplement the family income. It was hard, low paid, backbreaking work that would often lead to painful rheumatic joints in the washer's fingers and hands, and spinal deformities from hours spent bent over a wash tub pounding with the Dolly or the washboard.

In the late 1920s, a new system of laundering the clothes came into being – *The Bag Wash Shop*. Each customer would be given a sack, into which they would put their washing to be laundered, take the bag to the shop, where for a set sum of money the bundle would be washed *in the bag* and be ready for collection the next day.

York Hall Public Baths Building

The children who were old enough to carry the bag would be given the task, in turn, to take and collect the bag full of washing. It was not a favourite with them as they knew they would be berated by the proprietor who said that Granny Norton over-filled the bag. However, there were a lot of people in the family who needed clean clothes and Granny had to get the washing done as cheaply as she could.

On 5 November 1929 new public baths were opened by the then Duke and Duchess of York (later King George VI and Queen Elizabeth), and named *York Hall Public Baths* in the Duke and Duchess' honour. It is a red bricked building and apart from the public baths the establishment also boasted two swimming pools, Turkish baths, public baths and washhouse. It has undergone many changes over the years but is still a public venue today, as it is now a state of the art *Gym and Leisure Centre* with many facilities including a main and teaching swimming pool.

In the 30s a purchased ticket for 'the baths' was exchanged for a very small rough-surfaced towel and a small bar of lather-free soap! The baths were in individually numbered cubicles and were filled by an attendant operating the flow of hot and cold water to each individual bath remotely.

The Washhouse, as it came to be known, was very popular with locals. The women would go once a week with their dirty laundry to use the newly installed giant machines. You could, for a small extra charge, also use the new electric irons provided. The women took a real pride in getting their clothes clean, particularly their whites to as brilliant a white as possible. The finish was highly regarded with the women clientele casting a surreptitiously critical or envious eye over the other women's washing either side of them. *The Washhouse* was also a notorious place for gossip and passing on of news.

The children never realised when they were growing up how much hard work and love Granny and Granddad Norton put into helping to raise their grandchildren, and keeping the house in a clean orderly fashion was just one part of it, but if you asked any younger member of the family at the time they would not be appreciative of all the effort the adults of the family put into making a good home. The truth dawned when they had families of their own.

Once a year, there would be a very thorough spring clean of the house. All the children would be given extra 'spring cleaning tasks' – there were many groans as the extra chores were given out but they all got on with them in good natured fashion. One of the annual tasks was cleaning the Venetian blinds of each window. These were made of wooden slats that had to be taken apart to clean. The slats would be scrubbed until the wood looked like new and the webbing - great long lengths of it holding the slats together - would be washed thoroughly until there was not a speck of dirt to be seen. Once the individual parts were dry, then the long task of re-assembly would take place with sighs of relief all round once they were back in their rightful place at the appropriate window to hang for another year.

Most of the furniture was wooden – good, solid, serviceable chairs and tables that needed to be polished regularly. The beds had feather or flock mattresses and pillows which needed a regular and vigorous shaking to stop the downy feathers from sticking together in uncomfortable clumps. In that era, sheets and blankets were the usual bed covering for those that could afford them; duvets were a continental style, virtually unknown. Occasionally a family would make a quilted 'eiderdown' to go on top of blankets in cold weather. The feathers were obtained gradually from the local poultry outlets. Floors were often covered, again if you could afford it, with a scattering of rugs that needed to be taken outside and beaten regularly to remove dust and dirt. Buckets full of hot soapy water would be used to scrub the floors for there were no electrical appliances to make life easier for the housewife. The kitchen range (the forerunner to the modern cooker) would have to be regularly cleaned and after being scrubbed, a coating of black lead would be applied to finish. Joyce Devey, an aunt of mine, recalled doing this chore even in the 1940s. Her boyfriend Vic Deeks would often have to wait outside for her while she finished the job. And of course there was the door-step which was usually a polished crimson, re-polished at least once a week – eyed by every woman who passed by, and certainly by everyone crossing the threshold.

Many families in Bethnal Green did not have the home comforts that the Norton family enjoyed. Many homes, where the breadwinner was not in regular work, had only broken furniture and, in some homes, a packing case could be found instead of a table, with no rugs or other floor covering over the bare boards nor curtains at the windows. Often a mattress would be stuffed with straw which would encourage bed bugs. This was a grim hand to mouth period of time which had most of the next decade to run.

12

Another Ending and New Beginnings

As is now, the weather could be harsh in winter and the winter of 1928-29 was indeed a severe one. People trod warily in the streets with canvas overshoes to navigate the black ice on the pavements and roads. Influenza was once more on its rounds and Maggie Norton again succumbed to this at the beginning of February 1929.

All the children were taken to see a pantomime at a local hall unaware of how ill Maggie was. It was 7 February and Ted recalls a family member arrived at the hall in the interval to fetch them back early from the performance. They were puzzled, they knew Maggie was ill but were unaware that she was dying. Silently they hurried home along the darkened streets. When they arrived home it was a heavy brooding atmosphere that met them inside and a sombre faced Granny Norton asked them all to be very quiet and go into the front parlour. Then she took Margaret and Ted by the hand and led them up to their parents' bedroom. Quietly and slowly she walked up the stairs with them and ushered them into the room. The first thing that Margaret and Ted noticed was that all the family were gathered in the room. Margaret recalled looking at her mum lying in bed and thinking how brilliant her mother's eyes were. James, their dad, was sitting next to the bed holding his wife's hand tenderly in his. Granny guided both children gently forward towards their mother's bedside; Maggie kissed each of her children and asked them to promise to be good for their Gran. They were puzzled why they needed to make this promise as neither child realised how ill their mother was; she had often been ill before but had always recovered. As they looked around the room at their relatives' faces, they could see only a deep sadness etched on their features and felt afraid.

My dad (Ted) never went to another pantomime in his life. I think he loved his mother more deeply than he ever said. I can honestly say that always, when asked, his facial expression would soften and his eyes would take on a faraway look at the memory of her and he would praise his mother saying what a wonderful and lovely lady she had been. Margaret, who was thirteen at the time of her mother's death, told me that she could not recall how or when she and her brother were told that their mother had died or how long it took them to realise that she would never again play or laugh or be there for them. Margaret remembered sitting in a little square nearby thinking there could not be a God, because if there had been one surely he would not have let their mother die.

Death, until the advent of antibiotics, was never very far away. Many families suffered bereavement but the fact that it was an event that touched so many families did not make it any easier to bear. Margaret and Ted's memories of their mother's death illustrate a loved one's passing in that era and the emotions experienced by those left to grieve. Nowadays, people will sit down and gently speak to children if the child loses a parent or grandparent but this was not how grief was dealt with then. Children were meant to be seen and not heard so they were not encouraged to talk about their mother's death. It may sound harsh but that is how life was at that time.

As was usual for the period, the children were taken to be fitted for black clothes. Margaret looked down at the severe, unrelieved colour and thought about the lovely bright dresses her mother had made for her. The black cloth made Margaret look ill as she had a pale complexion and only added to her depressed appearance. She did not cry when her mother died, she did not cry until she returned home after the trip to purchase the mourning clothes. She had gone upstairs to her parent's rooms and found her mother's overall hanging behind the kitchen door. She told me how she cuddled it to her and breathed in the fragrant smell of her mother and cried as if her heart would break.

For several weeks after her mother's death, Margaret was very quiet and withdrawn, only wanting to play games on her own. Granny Norton watched over her anxiously. Margaret herself had been a sickly child, often in the past suffering from fainting attacks and for a while had been an out-patient of the local Children's Hospital.

One day Margaret, whilst playing alone in her room, had draped some material over her head like a scarf and looked into the mirror. Who knows what goes through the mind of a grieving child, but she suddenly screamed and when Granny Norton came running into the room she told her she had seen her mother looking back at her. Granny was a kind and sensible woman and while cuddling her told her gently that she should not keep looking into mirrors as only vain people did this.

Margaret described the events of 15 February, the day of her mother's funeral. There were only coaches and horses at that time. Maggie recalled sitting in the coach with the curtains closed. It felt strange to her to be sitting inside this coach as it jolted and jerked its way towards Manor Park Cemetery. The horses had set off at a sedate pace but once out of the district they were encouraged to trot which led to more violent jolting of the coach, making it hard for Maggie to concentrate not only on where she was going but why she was there. Her brother Ted clearly remembered the horses. They were black with manes combed glossy. They wore silver decorations on their bridles with large black plumes of feathers attached to the harness on their heads. Everywhere he looked that day, people were clothed in black; from then on he never liked black, it always reminded him of his beloved mother's untimely death.

For a while on Sundays, the children would be taken to visit the graves of Elizabeth and Maggie in Manor Park Cemetery to put flowers on the graves; a sad trip for young children to undertake but as time passed the visits became less frequent for the children as they were encouraged to join a Sunday School at the local church. The church was in an area highly populated by a Jewish community. These people spoke a little differently to the indigenous population but nonetheless were known to be hard working. Some opened shops selling unusual foodstuffs for that era such as pickled herrings and sausage and onion bread as well as goods from the continent. The church itself gave a new insight into life for the children with many activities they had not participated in before including the Junior Guild, which encouraged young people to join the choir or the drama group run by the Guild. Guilds such as these were a wonderful addition to children's lives in many parts of the East End and helped children from all walks of life to grow into well-rounded adults.

Young Ted was always keen to stand up and sing. Once, after Sunday school, they went to the Guild where a group of them were invited to sing, including young Ted, as always he put his heart and soul into the performance but near to the end of the song he felt the need to wipe his nose. Unfortunately the only piece of material he had on him was a rag in his pocket he had used in art class at school! On their return home that night, the family were told of young Ted and the painting rag that became his makeshift handkerchief (they all laughed).

Once a year, the Guild would enter the choir for a competition which was held in Essex Hall on The Strand. As the weeks wore on, the excitement would mount until finally the day of the competition arrived. After their performance,

Margaret recalled, they would hurry down to the Embankment Gardens to exuberantly run around letting out all the pent up energy from the weeks of hard work leading up to the competition. When they returned to the hall, they would be given tea while they waited for the results of the competition. One year they won the Shield and they returned home triumphant that night.

Each week, after church, the children would go to a Jewish bakery to buy bread. They would patiently wait in the queue to be served and looking around them would see the local women bringing in their dinners to be cooked in the bake-house ovens. Each dish would have a skewer with a numbered metal tag on it. The children loved these morning trips after Sunday school, passing through a busy market full of the sounds and smells of a variety of wares for sale.

In the year that Maggie died, two happy events also took place. 1929 saw the birth of Phoebe and Charlie Deeks' second child, a son who they named Victor (known to all as Vic). Again, as he had done at his daughter's birth in 1918, Charles purchased some wood (this time oak), and put it aside in his workshop to season until his son grew up and married. Skilled artisans such as Charles Deeks could be found into the 1960s still producing fine pieces of hand carved furniture.

Detail of the furniture carved by Charles Deeks

The second happy event was the marriage of James and Susannah's daughter Lydie. All the family were close as you would expect them to be. They all lived either in the same house or nearby and the friendship between Lydie and Ted Bates gradually turned to love. Lydie had helped her parents and brother-in-law with the raising of her sister's two boys, so was often in the company of Ted. The newly-weds lived nearby in the little flat above the office where Ted worked. In time, Lydie and Ted Bates were blessed with a child Susie, who was born in 1931. Susie was a bright, beautiful and vivacious child. Always full of fun like her cousins, she grew up in a different decade to her other cousins and siblings.

All James and Susannah's children were now married and they had eight surviving grandchildren, all were growing up fast. Around the time of Susie's birth this last photo of the couple was taken. Susannah still had a serene smile in spite of many sad events that must have clouded her life and James was still a fine figure of a man – clearly a devoted couple.

Ted recalls going on a trip with a boys' club to the seaside for a few days at about the same time. The children had always been taught to save for things and Ted had saved for his trip to the seaside. However, the pennies saved did not go as far as he had hoped. He wrote a postcard to his Dad, which said:

No mon, no fun, love your Son

In that era post would be delivered twice a day and the postcard duly arrived the next day. His dad thought it would not hurt Ted to be taught to wait, so he sent back a postcard with the words:

So sad, too bad, love your Dad

He then put a postal order in a second envelope for Ted and sent it in the next post. You can imagine the downcast look on Ted's face when he received the first postcard and then the delight when he received the postal order in the second delivery. Ted hurried to the local Post Office to change the postal order into money and sent his Dad a 'thank you' post card while he was there.

James Overy in 'Hogmanay' costume, note the fake sporran!!

As Ted grew older, his dad James Overy would take Ted to work with him for the day during the school holidays. James had a weekly list of customers that ordered from Charrington the Brewery for whom he still worked, as a drayman. He would wait for a long trip to the seaside before offering his son the chance of an outing with him for the day. Ted was always mad keen to go on these day-trips. He loved to sit and view the ever changing scenery as the horses trotted along the road. First he noticed the cobbled streets with rows of terraced houses as he went by the brewery yard, each with different curtains at the little uniform windows and the women out, each morning, sweeping their steps clean of any dirt while checking to see that their step was cleaner than their neighbours; likewise, polishing the brass door knocker until visitors could see the reflection of their face in it and not forgetting a quick scrutiny of the neighbour's door knocker to make sure their own was cleaner and shinier. Gradually the scenery would change and the houses became larger, set apart with little front gardens that could be admired through the boundary railings. James Overy was a keen gardener and liked to point out some of the different plants to his son.

Further into the journey, green fields would replace the streets with small houses or cottages often dotted about in hamlets. Ted was fascinated by how different the homes of these people appeared from the outside. James Overy loved to be out and about, he was a born mimic with a little bit of mischief in his character, sometimes they would pass a chicken farm and he would crow in imitation of a cockerel. All the hens would get into a fluster as they searched for the cockerel; short feathery wings flapping as they frantically ran around their pens, some even managing to get into the next pen, which made Ted laugh as he could see that all the different breeds were meant to be in their own pens and not mixed in together. Finally the sea would come into view and it would not be long before the horse and cart drew up at the customer's premises. Ted would jump down and help his dad unload the order they then had a hearty lunch followed by a stroll along the front before setting off for home.

Ted also recalled how his dad was able to mimic other animals; he once convinced a public house landlord that there was a cat trapped behind a cupboard, then quietly left as they struggled to move the cupboard to free the 'cat'!

The funniest incident was when James Overy and his friend, both keen football fans, managed to get tickets to see their team in an important away match. James and his friend travelled to Birmingham for the match and, after a thrilling game in which their team won, they were in good spirits so ready to celebrate. James was always a charismatic man who made friends very easily so by the end of the evening at the local public house James and his friend had made many new acquaintances. The landlord had enjoyed their company so much that as he said goodbye he added, "It has been great to meet you both and I will not forget you and hope you come back and see us sometime, although I expect you will soon forget us." James, never one to not rise to a challenge, said of course they would not forget. The landlord repeated that they would always be welcome and not forgotten.

James and his friend returned home on the train and planned a 'surprise' trip back in a couple of months. James set about gathering some 'props' for the return visit which included two Homburg hats that he 'tailored to fit the occasion' by pushing up the 'dent' in the crown, usually part of the hat style, and trimming down the brim of the hat as a Jewish tailor would wear. He acquired two black coats, false beards and a tray with a neck-strap. On the tray he put matches, shoes laces, pipe cleaners and other sundry items. Satisfied with their disguises they set off on the train to Birmingham. Now, James Overy was not only a good animal and bird mimic but, he was an excellent mimic of other people's accents and living in London gave him lots of opportunities to listen and learn a variety of speech inflections. They arrived at the public house just at opening time and made their way into the 'public' bar with James offering his tray of 'saleable' wares to the customers. No one recognized the two apparently 'Jewish' gentlemen and, as their zealous selling tactics were not appreciated by the customers, the landlord firmly asked them to leave. Undeterred, they entered the 'saloon' bar of the public house where again they were disruptive.

The landlord was angry to see them again and threatened to call the police. At this point James and his friend took off their disguises – "I knew you would forget us!" said a beaming James.

The landlord was amazed and delighted to see them and gave them a great night out to make up for not recognising them!

13

The Great Depression Years

Many countries were in debt from the cost of borrowing incurred during World War One, including Great Britain which had also been forced to sell off foreign assets to assist with the cost of the war. The damage to the European economy by manpower losses, the upsetting of Continental markets due to German Reparations, all the many dangerous stock marketing activities in North America, even the depredations of the Influenza pandemic provided the soup for a global economic disaster. As recent events have shown, no-one seemed to see catastrophe approaching. The financial cost of the war to the whole of the economy of Europe was staggering and those debts left many nations with fragile economies throughout the 1920-30s. By 1921, Britain's recovery from the 'Great War' began to suffer from a domestic slump and unemployment started to rise – so much for the government's promise to returning soldiers at the end of the conflict that they would give them 'Homes fit for heroes'. In East London the failure of local industries to cope with the economic challenges of the time led many of the people of the area into unemployment with Bethnal Green being one of the areas blighted by this.

The Great Depression officially began in America where share prices had been falling since early September 1929 but the U.S. stock market finally crashed on 29 October, forever known as 'Black Tuesday'. The American economic collapse had a profound knock on effect for many nations. The Great Depression in Europe and beyond began in 1930 but lasted many years, indeed not all countries came out of the depression until the 1940s. Some European countries fared worse than others. For example German unemployment and inflation rose steeply leading to serious widespread disturbances and indirectly encouraged many German citizens to vote for the Nazi and Communist Parties.

In Great Britain, following pressure from the Labour Government's allies, as well as the Liberals and the Conservative opposition, the Committee on National Expenditure, chaired by Sir George May, was set up to suggest ways in which expenditure could be curbed. The May Report was published in July 1931 and it recommended that public sector wages and benefits would need to be cut together with an increase in taxation to balance the country's books during the recessionary climate. However, in a 25 page memorandum dated January 1930, a junior government minister – Oswald Mosley – had suggested that the Government should take control of banking and exports together with increasing pensions to boost spending and thereby ameliorate the growing problem of unemployment. He was supported by several prominent political figures including the well-known East End radical George Lansbury. When Mosley's ideas were turned down he left the labour Party and formed the *New Party* which failed to win seats in the 1931 General Election. As a result he was forced to seek inspiration elsewhere.

Following a visit to Italy, Mosley eventually went on to form the BUF (British Union of Fascists). At first many prominent Jewish businessmen supported this party as it was known to be opposed to communism but by late 1932 anti-Semitism had crept into its doctrine and the party speeches became full of disparaging remarks about the Jews being allegedly untrustworthy as they were accused of being key players in both Communism and Capitalism. The BUF's remit was to protect national interests and they maintained that the Jewish population was an international body which had no loyalty to Great Britain.

The BUF wore uniforms of black shirt and trousers to which military style boots were added later. In 1933 they opened an East London office at 64 Squirries Street (off Bethnal Green Road). Being proud of their Party they decorated the premise window with the party's newly devised symbol – a bolt of lightning within a circle – which became known locally as 'the flash in the pan'. A clever parody on the old military term for a misfire and the notion of something not lasting very long.

East London at that time had the largest Jewish population in Great Britain, which had been greatly increased in 1933 due to a substantial influx of people of Jewish descent seeking refuge within these shores to escape anti-Jewish sentiment in Germany. The BUF played on the fears of local small businesses. With the lack of heavy industry in the area, the trade unions were weak, giving the BUF the opportunity to whip up resentment towards many Jewish-owned businesses. The BUF held many open air meetings in this period in Victoria Park as well as other local venues with violent, stage managed heckling, and missile hurling, all designed to convince locals there was a common enemy to be overcome.

The announcement that Mosley and his Black-shirts (as they were known) planned a bold and provocative march through the East London areas of Shoreditch, Limehouse, Bow and Bethnal Green on 4 October 1936 was greeted with anger and a determination that it should be stopped. A petition was signed and local politicians tried to have the march called off – but to no avail.

On the day of the planned march, up to 250,000 people gathered to 'defend' the East End. As the police tried to clear a path for the marchers, the protesters fought back vigorously, a barricade, made of a builder's lorry, barrels, corrugated iron and lengths of timber, was thrown across the path of the marchers to prevent them from entering Cable Street, one of the narrowest thoroughfares of the planned route. People in their houses threw eggs, milk bottles and the contents of chamber pots from upstairs windows, whilst people in the streets threw marbles under the police horses' hooves. The march could not proceed and Mosley was ordered to abandon his plans. He complied with this order as he felt he should not disobey the Metropolitan Police Commissioner. It was a blow against fascism and that night there was dancing in the streets.

Ted recalled the feeling of great tension during the build up to this event. People listened to news on the 'wireless' of the planned march and had gathered to discuss, often in small groups, the motives of the BUF. As each day passed and the time drew nearer to the date of the march, the streets took on a determined air of resistance with the desire to stop fascism and its ideals and when lawful protest failed they repulsed it by physical force – street democracy appeared to triumph over fascism that day – well that is one view of the events but it would seem that mob rule was the actual victor. The victory was brief, however, and in 1937 the BUF stood in the LCC elections gaining 23% of the vote in Bethnal Green. Again this was a short lived victory as the tide finally turned against the BUF and its beliefs with the outbreak of World War Two.

During the period of 'the Depression' southern England was not as badly affected as the North where most of the heavy industries producing goods for export were situated. In fact, during these bleak years many areas of southern England, including Bethnal Green, London, witnessed a housing boom.

There were, of course, queues of unemployed outside the offices of the Board of Guardians in Bethnal Green as there were in other parts of East London during the Depression. Each borough council and Poor Law Union was required to levy their own rates but it was an unfair system that meant the 'poorer' boroughs were penalised as they had to set a higher rate in order to fund the Poor Relief in the borough (this benefit was paid out of the rates at that time by the borough council to residents of the borough, thus more affluent boroughs with little poor relief liability were able to set lower rates).

Early in 1921, Poplar Council took the decision to challenge this unfair anomaly by suggesting that as poor relief was a problem for the whole of London, then all boroughs should share the cost of poor relief. Marches were organised in support of these councillors when they refused to levy their borough's rates that year. In July of that year, 36 councillors were served writs and summoned to appear in court charged with contempt. All the local boroughs followed the case with interest. At the end of the proceedings, the councillors were instructed to levy the rate within 14 days or face imprisonment but they remained defiant and consequently were arrested and sent to prison. Public support for them grew while they languished behind bars; many of the surrounding boroughs were in defiant mood including Bethnal Green which passed a resolution to withhold the levy unless the prisoners were released. The outcome of this affair was an agreement to pool all the costs of poor relief and spread it out evenly amongst the London boroughs. But the victory was short lived as the recession deepened, forcing the inevitable rate rise to meet the borough's financial commitments.

The government had promised money to fund a scheme to provide work on slum clearance for ex-servicemen, but became suspicious that the funds would not be used to provide ex-servicemen with work so they withdrew the offer.

Many families were still living in overcrowded conditions although families by the early 1930s were on average smaller than previous decades. There had been earlier Housing Acts and some slum clearance in the 1920s but further Acts in 1930-

1935 recognised that in some areas housing was of very poor quality, with acute overcrowding and poor sanitation. The government of the day embarked upon a job creating programme through the LCC led by Herbert Morrison with the slogan: *Up with the houses! Down with the slums!*

During the 1930s, the London County Council identified several clearance sites in Bethnal Green, amongst them Pritchard's Road (near where Susannah had been born in Ann's Place), although work did not start on this until 1933 when finances became available. Further slum clearance work commenced in 1934 on the sites of Ada Place, Hollybush Gardens, Potts Street and Delta Street. The local council had identified many other smaller sites but these were at the time considered by the LCC to be too small for redevelopment.

However, the LCC built the Pritchard Estate which consisted of two blocks of flats named Ada House and Pritchard House in the late 1930s as part of the slum clearance and rebuild programme so the name of the original builder, Pritchard, was for the time being kept as a reminder of his family's historic ownership of land in that area.

Other sites earmarked for redevelopment in 1935 included the area around Pedley Street where 353 people had lived in 85 houses. By 1936 the LCC undertook clearance and redevelopment on a much larger scale when they took the decision to target the area around Cambridge Heath Road from the border with Hackney to Old Bethnal Green Road and Bethnal Green Hospital; from the west, Pritchard's Road and Temple Street and from the east Lark Row and Russia Lane. This large area had contained 1,210 properties which were a mix of 693 working class houses, 183 flats in Peabody Buildings, 134 flats over shops, 59 factories, 54 commercial premises, a school, a church, 12 public houses and a population of 5,471. Eight more areas were designated for slum clearance in 1937 – Minerva Street, Emma Street, Vyner

Street, Tent Street, Coopers Gardens, Herald Street, Turin Street and finally Squirries Street. There had been earlier work to clear slums in the 1920s, a good example being the Collingwood Estate built on the site between Brady Street and Collingwood Street, a total of five acres.

Apart from the LCC's efforts to improve living conditions, private enterprises were also undertaken during these years of which these examples are a few; *The Nag's Head Field* was designated as a clearance area in 1933. The Nag's Head Housing Society then started building flats north of Shipton Street and west of Ropley Street. These were completed in 1937 with a second phase of building taking place to the west and bounded by Ravenscroft Street in 1939. The Bethnal Green and East London Housing Association (formed 1926) by an Industrial Housing Fellowship Group, opened its first block of 15 flats – the four-storeyed Queen Margaret Flats in St. Jude's Road. In 1931 The Association had issued – AN APPEAL TO CHRISTIAN PEOPLE – for funds to aid slum clearance and the building of basic good quality housing was delivered with a vivid description of life in the slums in a typical street with multiple occupancy of houses:

It has a stable for horses on the ground floor. Directly above, if we climb a staircase, or what was once a staircase, we find two families. Only a wooden floor separates them from the animals below. There is no privacy, for the stair to the floor above also enters the room. The gas is burning, though it is brilliantly light outside, because the window has been blocked up, owing to there being no glass, and nothing to keep the winter chill out. Upstairs we go again, here we find two more families, a little better off, for here they have windows, but they have to be propped up when any wind comes along, for fear lest they should fall into the street below, or into the room. Thirteen adults, twelve children, and some horses! Perhaps there are not many rooms left over stables as bad as this, but the scandal is that there should be any. How can one keep one's self-respect, one's pride in one's home, under conditions like that? How can the wife be bright, and keep the place tidy when there is no privacy, when other people's children are continually bringing dirt into her place? Isn't it sufficient to tempt any man to crime in order to try and do something to get a better home? Home. What a ghastly misuse of that word, for often it is a home for the rats and the bugs.

The aim of all the housing societies was to give families decent living conditions and pride in themselves and their homes.

Photographs of accommodation built by The East End Dwelling Company give examples of the variety of domestic dwellings for which they were responsible.

The East End Dwellings Co., a philanthropic society, built Mulberry House in 1934. The building of 10 flats in Coventry Street for Allen & Hanbury, tenements and workshops at the corner of Cheshire and Menotti Streets, was another private undertaking as was a block on the site of nos. 34-40 Viaduct Street for the Seabright Estate, a four-storeyed brick and concrete building on the site of nos. 107-109 Cambridge Road by S. Leapman, all in 1936, and 24 flats in Cheshire Street by New Era Estates in 1937.

During these years of depression and regeneration, Ted and Margaret were nearing adulthood and, like many young people during this period, were starting to experience some of the joys and pitfalls that pre-adulthood could bring.

When Ted entered his teens he reached a milestone in his life when his father sent him to a local Jewish tailor to have his first suit with full length trousers made. Oh the excitement at having a grown up suit! His cousins Jimmy and Eddy accompanied him to the tailor's shop to choose the material and to be measured. The tailor welcomed them inside, it was a small shop with very little natural light as the windows in the shop front were tiny and to augment the lighting the tailor had installed fluorescent strip lights but these gave a bluish light.

The tailor listened to young Ted's request for a dark blue suit and got down a bale of what looked like the required colour. Ted delighted with his choice, patiently stood still while the tailor took all the necessary measurements. A few weeks later the three youngsters returned to collect the suit. It was a perfect fit and both he and his cousins were very impressed – until they left the shop. Outside, in natural light, the dark blue material showed its true 'purple' colour.

Suits were always a serviceable and conservative colour - no man or boy wore 'purple' in the first half of the 20th Century. Ted was aghast and went back into the shop to complain but the Jewish tailor smiled benignly and said he could do nothing as Ted had chosen the material.

Ted trailed home slowly with a dejected air, thinking his Dad would have some sympathy. But James Overy knew this would be an important lesson for his son. He gently but firmly pointed out to his son that he had chosen the material and should have asked to take the cloth outside if it was too dark in the shop to see it properly. He also said that he could not afford another suit so quickly for his son so he would have to wear it. Poor Ted was downhearted at his Dad's apparent lack of help and understanding, although in later years he did admit he was grateful for the lesson learned from this episode – for the rest of his life he always checked things properly – especially colours!

Naturally all Ted's peers thought the suit colour hilarious and Ted had to endure much teasing. After a week or so he hatched a plan. He and his cousins left the house for a 'walk' in the Park. Once inside the gates an 'enthusiastic' game of football was played which resulted in the suit trousers that Ted was wearing that day getting badly torn. This appeared to Ted and his cousins a good result as the trousers were beyond repair. Ted was again punished with sitting on the chair in the window – but he did not mind as he had got rid of that frightful suit.

While Ted was experiencing 'the suit episode', his sister had reached school leaving age and was off to attend her first job interview. There was no guidance given by the schools on careers or even how to conduct yourself at an interview when children reached school leaving age but Aunt Lottie had offered to go with her. Margaret was grateful for the support as she took her first tentative steps towards adulthood and working life.

Since Margaret enjoyed sewing she thought she would be happy training as a milliner; when her mother was alive,

Margaret found watching her mother create a hat, fascinating. However, the position being offered was at a factory specialising in the creation of artificial flowers but Margaret thought that sounded rather a nice profession to enter. At the end of the interview Margaret accepted the job and Aunt Lottie and young Margaret were shown into a large room where the flowers were produced.

The room had a long table at which sat approximately a dozen young women on either side, the forewoman sitting at the head of the table, was a small neat lady with a sharp tongue! No talking was allowed during working hours nor were you allowed any tea breaks, however mugs of tea were put on the table in front of each girl so she could drink while she worked. Margaret found flower production interesting as she loved flowers, but as she was only a junior member of staff her job was to cut lengths of cotton covered wires. After she had cut twenty, she had to stitch them together and then making sure they remained as a bundle she would dip them in a glue pot. Once these sprays of stems were dry, she had to take the bunch in hand and pull one stem gently in a downwards curve and attach a little gauze leaf, then repeat the process with each stem in the bunch until she had a balanced bouquet of leafy stems ready for the flowers to be attached. The ends of the stem wires were sharp and often by the end of the day Margaret would have cuts to her hands from these.

Margaret would often be given the chance to deliver samples to various customers and this she said she thoroughly enjoyed. However, there were mundane errands to be undertaken as well and Margaret recalled one such errand that nearly landed her in trouble. Margaret was a quiet, shy, young lady and naturally a little in awe of the older members of the staff.

On this particular day, Margaret had a list of items to obtain, she had also been asked by a fellow worker to fetch some milk in a cup. As it was raining, Margaret tried to keep the cup covered as much as possible on her return journey to the factory. However, as she climbed the metal staircase to the factory door she slipped and cracked the bottom of the cup. Margaret was horrified as she saw the milk slowly drip from the base of the cup, but thought that as it was dripping very, very slowly she might be able to pass the cup to the owner before they realised that the cup was damaged. For the rest of the day, Margaret waited for a raised voice from the cup owner but none came. Perhaps the owner thought she herself had broken it.

The factory owners employed an elderly man whose job it was to supply the workers with empty boxes and remove the full boxes of finished flowers. He was a man of few words, so one day when he suddenly turned and addressed the girls working at the table they were all instantly attentive.

"Don't make a sound," he said in a firm but moderate voice.

Margaret nervously looked up at the foreman and then turned her head slowly to see what he was staring at – to her horror she saw an enormous rat scurrying along the shelf! Margaret, like her mother, could not abide vermin, so for the rest of the day she was terrified the rat would put in another appearance.

As she journeyed home that night she felt sick with the fear of further sightings of the rat or, worse rats!

Margaret soon began to pray hard each night for a means to escape the artificial flower factory and, suddenly, her prayers were answered. A friend who knew Margaret's Gran was worried about Margaret working in a factory with vermin running around, offered Margaret the chance to learn tailoring. Better still, Margaret found the premises were very near to home as well as giving her the chance to enhance her sewing skills. This job was the happiest and most rewarding time of Margaret's working life.

In this new job, people were allowed to talk while they worked and Margaret was to meet Annie here, who became from then on her lifelong friend.

1932 heralded a great change in the lives of the Nortons for this was the year their beloved Granny Norton died. The woman who had given so much to the care and well-being of her family and had been the core of the family for as long as they could remember was suddenly no longer with them.

Ted said that for a time it felt like a void had opened in their lives, but gradually they all began to pick up their lives and go forward. Lydie and Lottie, the daughters of James and Susannah, and their families still lived in rooms at 49 Approach Road as did their son-in-law James Overy with his children. This must have been a great comfort to James Norton, having lost the woman he had shared his life with for so many years.

The year of 1932 was the year young Ted left school. He was 14 years old, the legal school leaving age. He was a bright young lad and managed to become apprenticed with a local electrical firm. How fortunate he was, not only because he was in full time employment learning a useful trade, but this trade probably served to save his life during the Second World War.

There was another family bereavement within two years with the sudden illness then death of young Jimmy. Ted and Jimmy were very close in every way; they were cousins, best friends and soul mates who looked after each other. This closeness was often found in families at this time, no doubt due to extended families often living in accommodation in the same road or at least nearby. Jimmy being the quiet reserved member of the family was glad to have young Ted by his side and Ted, being two years younger than Jimmy looked up to his older cousin with genuine affection and enjoyed the camaraderie they had. They were perfectly matched, one being introvert and the other extrovert. Jimmy at one time thought he would boost his self-confidence by purchasing a set of dumb-bells to hopefully fill out his lean body with some muscles but sadly he managed to knock himself out the first time he tried lifting these by attempting to lift a really heavy weight. Ted was sympathetic telling Jimmy not to worry because he was fine as he was, as far as Ted was concerned.

Jimmy's illness had started with a painful leg. He saw a local doctor who sent him for tests which led eventually to him being given an appointment at one of the big London hospitals. The doctor at the hospital ordered further tests but then came the day the results were given to Jimmy – he had a cancerous tumour in his leg. The doctors tried hard to save him, even amputating his leg but he lost his battle for life on 24 January 1934; with cruel irony this was sixteen years to the day since his father had lost his life in the Great War. All the family grieved deeply at the loss of such a young life. He was just seventeen when he died, but two members of the family were particularly affected by the untimely passing of Jimmy. Ted was grief stricken to have lost his beloved cousin and Lydia was heartbroken to have lost her big brother.

14

Pre-World War Two years

As the decade of the 1930s progressed, events that would ultimately affect the world at large were taking shape. People were beginning to question how their country should be governed. The hijacking of such debates gave opportunity for movements such as Communism – the halcyon notion of everyone being equal – and Fascism, directed towards the State being the great provider. Both doctrine steered away from the concept of democracy. Democracy, where it was entrenched, was reacting by bringing in universal suffrage. In Germany, Adolf Hitler was appointed Chancellor in 1933, having gained leadership of a coalition government in the German Parliament, an event which was ultimately to have a profound effect on world history over the next twelve years and beyond.

Although these were worrying times for everyone, with considerable unemployment, growing militancy and unease at events unfolding in Europe, 'ordinary' people still carried on their day to day living.

Meanwhile, within the extended family and friends, Margaret had met Albert Smith whilst working at the Co-Operative Society. Margaret and Bert (as he became known) started to save towards the day they would marry. Margaret said young couples would save like mad towards their future life together, to buy furniture and although like most couples living at that time they would be renting a home, they would still dream of their future life together. Lack of money, combined with their wish to be together, caused them to search for rather gentle pleasures by today's standards. But it seems they were content to stroll through Victoria Park or sit chatting in the upstairs front room, watching their world go by outside and just simply being together – 'courting'.

Margaret was not the only member of the family who started courting. Her father, James Overy, obviously missed his wife and since his mother-in-law's death must have found life lacking in many ways – he especially missed his mother-in-law's cooking, he told his friends. He had met one or two ladies over the years but none of these friendships ever blossomed into more than just casual acquaintances. His children were growing up and putting out their own tentative steps on life's path. His wife's family were still close-knit, but I suspect he felt rather alone at times even in a crowded room.

James Overy announced to his two children one day at the dinner table that he had a while before met a woman by the name of Elizabeth Carter. She had been a widow for a number of years and her only child had died when a baby. He said that he would like Margaret and Ted to meet this woman as he was thinking of re-marrying. I don't think it had occurred to either Margaret or Ted that their dad would marry again and that they would have a step-mother. They were both rather shocked at this news and were unable to imagine anyone ever taking the place of their beloved mother in their family. Even so, James said he would like them to meet Elizabeth so he would be taking them all to the seaside for an outing the following Sunday.

The day dawned bright and sunny and the three of them set off to meet Elizabeth at the station. As they drew near to the station entrance James suddenly raised an arm in welcome to Elizabeth who nervously smiled back pleased to see them all. James introduced them to each other and the children politely shook hands with this short, stout, heavy featured woman.

They boarded the train to Ramsgate and sat opposite their Dad and Elizabeth. Elizabeth was probably just as nervous at meeting them and tried to draw them out by asking all sorts of questions about their likes and dislikes. They arrived at their destination and after a walk along the sea front James asked Margaret and Ted if they would like to go off for a walk on their own for a while. They readily jumped at the chance to go and be themselves without this stranger watching them. Ted and Margaret walked along the seafront and started to swap their first impressions of Elizabeth, both were understandably a little uneasy at the thought of this woman expecting them to call her 'mother' if their dad married her.

One January day, just before the annual staff Co-Operative Grand Ball, Margaret woke to find she had a sore throat. People occasionally have a sore throat, it will soon pass she thought. However, on this occasion it did not and soon a red rash appeared. Margaret, at her dad's insistence, had to visit the doctor who diagnosed scarlet fever.

Before Margaret could take in the news of what her illness was, she found an ambulance had arrived at the surgery to take her to hospital. Margaret was distraught at being admitted to hospital – after all she had not even felt that ill and a hospital stay would mean she would miss the annual ball that she had been looking forward so much to attending.

Margaret was treated in hospital for three weeks – three *long* weeks in her memory – before she was transferred to a convalescent home in Dartford.

Until some years after World War Two, patients with serious illnesses or injuries would often finish their treatment at a convalescent home. The journey must have seemed long to the patients as they could see little out of the ambulance windows. When they alighted from the ambulance they saw the 'Home', a typically large, red brick building set in pleasant grounds enclosed by elegant railings.

Once inside the home they saw there were a number of cubicles on either side of a long corridor. Each patient was assigned a cubicle to take a bath and were then given a bundle of clothes to wear. Margaret was aghast as she opened her bundle to find some very old fashioned attire. Margaret could not believe the sight of the navy blue serge cami-knickers with a button to attach them to the white camisole. The outer dress also of a navy blue serge material, had a sailor style collar; to finish the ignominious outfit off was a pair of thick black stockings. What a shock after the pretty feminine clothes young Margaret had grown used to wearing! Once dressed they were taken by another ambulance to a different building and allotted beds in a large dormitory.

Each day a bell would be rung to summon the convalescents to rise for meals etc. The time seemed to drag slowly to Margaret and she was glad to escape to the grounds whenever she was able to for a breath of fresh air and a walk in the gardens. As this particular convalescent home was for patients who had contracted contagious illnesses, no visitors were allowed, so many an hour was filled with the sending and receiving of letters to families and friends. Margaret enjoyed letter writing and sent a stream of letters to her family and friends including her Bert and, she must have be keen to hear back from them with news from what for her an 'outside' world.

The day came for what she hoped was a final examination she said later how thrilled she was when the doctor, after checking her, pronounced her free from contagion. She could return home.

Before departure convalescents had to undergo a discharge process. Margaret dressed herself in her own clothes and said goodbye to the hideous attire she had been forced to wear. Margaret's Aunt Lottie met her at the gates and the two women hugged one another after such a long enforced absence. They chatted and laughed non-stop on the long tram ride home. The whole family welcomed Margaret back with great enthusiasm, especially her dad and her brother Ted, who had missed her enormously.

In 1935, James Overy married Elizabeth Carter (or 'Lizzie', as she was referred to by her family and friends). The children were among the guests present at the church wedding. Lizzie did not want to set up home in Approach Road as it had been the home James had shared with his first wife. Instead, at Lizzie's suggestion, they moved to a little terraced house in Victoria Street, Leyton, only a few miles away so many visits could be made back to Approach Road.

Ted and Maggie were both sad to leave the lovely large house in Approach Road, the only home they had known throughout their lives but they knew they could always return to see their Norton relations and often did so as the bond between them all remained very strong. Indeed, many years later both Ted and Margaret would often recall their happy childhood memories of Bethnal Green. It would appear that you could take the person out of Bethnal Green but not Bethnal Green out of the person.

It was not uncommon for widows or widowers to remarry and set up a new home together and for the children of the earlier marriages to live with them. No matter what the children might feel, they usually did not wish to hurt the feelings of their remaining parent; besides, during that era until you married you would usually stay at home. Ted had reluctantly left his electrical apprenticeship within a year of his father's remarriage. He had been 'encouraged' to do so by Lizzie as she felt he could earn a better wage if he took employment elsewhere. He commenced employment with Bass Mitchell and Butler (who in 1967 merged with Charrington) working as an office clerk but never lost his enthusiasm for electrical work.

Lizzie was an accomplished tailoress who worked for a bespoke Jewish tailors as an out worker. There were many such family-run businesses owned by Jewish families at that time in East London. A delivery of partially completed suits would regularly arrive at the little house in Leyton for Lizzie to finish. Any completed work would, at the same time, be collected and paid for. The skill required to undertake this work was not financially recognised though, for the hourly rates were extremely low which often, though not always, led to bitterness within the community against the Jewish owners of these businesses.

One day, Ted had an accident and broke his leg, Lizzie, determined to fulfil her duties as a step-mother asked Margaret to take back both partially completed and finished suits to the tailoring company with a message explaining that as her step-son had broken his leg she would not be able to undertake any further work until he was properly recovered. The Jewish owner was very concerned to hear of Ted's accident and wished him well. The next time Margaret saw the owner, he asked after her brother enquiring, "How are the fingers now on your brother's foot?" This question, when repeated at home, caused much mirth in the family. But the humour was affectionate, local respect was very strong.

Although outgoing in most aspects of his character Ted could, as a teenager, be shy at times and one such incident was when Lizzie insisted on accompanying him to the hospital for his appointment to have his broken leg examined. Ted found Lizzie a little loud compared to his quiet reserved mother and as he stood nervously at the bus stop with Lizzie, waiting with the young women officer workers, he fervently hoped that the bus would arrive before Lizzie could say anything to embarrass him.

Luck appeared to be with him that day as the bus soon pulled up at the stop. The young women office workers perhaps felt sorry for the tall, good looking young man with his leg in plaster and ensured he was given the last available seat on the bus. Ted timidly thanked them and, once he got himself as comfortable as possible, cautiously looked to see where his step-mother was. Lizzie had been swept to the very front of the bus. Seeing Ted look her way, she waved to him.

"All right son?" followed her loud and dreaded voice.

Ted must have cringed.

Then she added as an afterthought, "I think I will get your father a nice piece of 'addock for his tea."

She had meant this as a kindly thought, but Ted told me much later that he remembered his face turning scarlet with embarrassment, as the young women all tried to hide their giggles behind their hands – and failed.

In 1936, Granddad Norton died. He had outlived his beloved wife by just a few years and although he found great comfort in his close family, especially those who remained in the house, he obviously missed his Susannah very much. He passed away peacefully and was buried with Susannah in Manor Park Cemetery.

Rose Ellis and John Deeks married in 1936. In the following year their daughter Barbara was born. Rose's family had not approved of the marriage so Barbara grew up not knowing her dad's family. As an adult she became a well-known actress under her professional name of Barbara Windsor, She did, some years later, meet one of her relatives, Gloria Parker when Barbara appeared on the BBC programme '*Who Do you Think You are?*'

Life is always full of good and bad, happy and sad events and the year before war was declared saw two family weddings. Lydia, like her cousin Margaret, had been courting for a while and early in 1938 Lydia and George Atkins were married, followed by Margaret and Bert Smith a little later in the year. Both brides-to-be had thrown themselves into their wedding plans with great excitement

Margaret recalled all the planning, booking the hall, arranging the details at the church, choosing the wedding flowers. She described it all with such pleasure to me one day, over a cup of tea; it was almost as if she could see it all again in her mind as it had happened. The young couple were lucky to have found a little flat and looked forward to starting married life there.

As the wedding day drew near it was customary at that time to arrange a little gathering of work mates and to offer them drinks and little snacks. Margaret had a friend at work who was also getting married so they decided to combine their pre-wedding events. The two young ladies passed trays of drinks and nibbles around their work mates, enduring much good natured teasing as they walked from table to table and floor to floor. At last, their social duties fulfilled, Margaret and her friend decided to make good their escape via a back exit rather than face more teasing by leaving through the front entrance. Quietly they crept down the fire escape stairs only to be 'surprised' by colleagues raining split peas down on the two of them. The girls fled giggling, and ran to Margaret's Grandmother Overy, who lived nearby. The old lady opened the door to find her granddaughter and friend standing on the step wriggling and laughingly asking if they could come in and remove the split peas from inside their clothing. Granny Overy thought this episode very comical and happily invited them in to remove the offending dried peas.

And so the day of Margaret and Bert's wedding dawned. Margaret's bridesmaids helped to dress her. Her dad was quite emotional and proud at the sight of his beautiful daughter in her wedding finery and no doubt the sight of his daughter that day must have brought back memories of his first wife and their own wedding day.

151

All the rest of the family departed for the church leaving just the bride and the bride's father. They waited for their turn to be collected and taken to the church but, after a while, when no one arrived to transport them Margaret naturally became anxious. Eventually they arrived at the church and Margaret and Bert were duly married but not before the vicar had started the ceremony with the wrong names for the bride and the groom.

Memorable mistakes continued as later that day at the couple's wedding reception, Margaret learned that half the guests had been originally taken to the wrong church, once that error had been realised more time was then lost transferring the guests to the right church; this had been the reason for the delay in collecting the bride and her father. The best laid plans, as they say, do not always work out smoothly.

Margaret and Albert set off on their honeymoon to Bournemouth the next day. It was a wonderful holiday but rumours of eventual war could be heard everywhere, making life and their future seem very uncertain. Although people were now living in turbulent times, life went on with great news for the family when Lydia and George's baby was born on 29 May 1939. Many years later Lydia wrote me a letter telling of her memories of her son's birth.

Lydia had to have an operation after baby George's birth and when she regained consciousness from the anaesthetic the nurses asked who the baby's 'Uncle Jim' was. Lydia replied that Jim was her long dead brother and she must have been dreaming of him. No doubt she was sad that her brother could not be there to see his nephew. She also told me of two strange coincidences – her father and her brother had both been born on a 29 May and both men had died on a 24 January.

15

The Start of World War Two,
The Phoney War and its Aftermath

ittle by little news from Europe of the threat of another
possible global conflict occupied the nation's thoughts.
Germany had been resentful, even before Hitler came to
power, of the punitive terms of the Versailles Treaty and
Germany's territorial losses. With Hitler in power rearmament
became more blatant. Feverish diplomatic attempts were made
in order to avoid a further conflict and the week of 21 August
1939 was one of great suspense when people became suddenly
aware of the Soviet-German pact. Events were clearly leading
towards war. Then the news reached the UK that German tanks
had rolled into northern and western Poland on 1 September.
People realised the inevitable was about to happen – the British
Government declared war on Germany on 3 September 1939
after the expiry of Chamberlain's ultimatum.

Three days before war was officially declared, members of
the public were ordered to maintain a blackout from dusk to
dawn and stick brown paper tape in the form of diagonal
crosses over the window panes to reduce injury from flying
glass. Women started to make blackout curtains for the
windows. Citizens could be heavily fined if even a tiny beam
of light was able to escape through a carelessly drawn curtain
during the hours of darkness. ARP (Air Raid Precautions)
wardens regularly patrolled the streets checking for any chink
of light, although usually for a first offence a warning would
be given. Both men and women were recruited for this work

and could easily be recognised by their standard blue overalls and tin hat inscribed with the letters ARP. The blackout officially came into being on the night of 1 September when all street lights were extinguished. Orders were issued for car headlights and bike lights not to be switched on during the hours of darkness resulting in many accidents as people tripped over kerb stones or bumped into lamp posts.

ARP wardens also controlled and issued Anderson and Morrison shelters as well as gas masks to the community. Shelters were duly issued and erected in as many dwellings with gardens or backyards as quickly as possible. Anderson shelters were a half circle shape made of sheets of corrugated steel bolted together with a door at the front; the back was a single sheet of corrugation. The shelters were 6ft (1.8 m) high, 4ft 6 in (1.4 m) wide, and 6ft 6 in (2 m) long. A trench at least 4ft feet deep would need to be dug prior to erecting the shelter and earth would be piled up and over the back, sides and roof of the shelter to a minimum depth of 15in (0.4m) to give further strength and protection. Anderson shelters were issued free of charge to all householders who earned less than £5 a week, those with a higher income were charged £7. These shelters could tolerate the violent ground movements when bombs landed nearby and so were much safer than concrete and brick constructed shelters that could and did collapse when the earth shook under an explosion. The downside to these structures was that they were very cold and damp, even prone to flooding in wet weather, becoming less attractive to people when night raids became more frequent. Nonetheless they probably did save a great deal of lives.

The other type of shelter was the Morrison shelter, designed for indoor use especially for people who did not live in accommodation with a cellar or basement or a garden.

The shelters arrived in D.I.Y assembly packs that had 359 parts plus 3 tools for assembly. They were approximately 6ft

6 in (2 m) long, 4ft (1.2 m) wide and 2ft 6 in (0.75 m) high, had a solid 1/8 in (3mm) steel-plate 'table top', welded wire mesh sides and a floor area big enough to take a double mattress. Once assembled, they resembled a large rabbit hutch. These shelters were issued free to those families applying for them whose income was less than £400 per annum. They were designed for a double mattress to fit inside so that people often slept in them in case of a sudden air raid. The principle was that they were strong enough to hold the rubble of a collapsed house with enough space for air, so that those inside would survive long enough to be dug out.

Barbara Nichol, an eight year old child at the start of this new terrifying conflict, remembers the family's Morrison shelter. At night as soon as the siren sounded, Barbara's mum would hurriedly take Barbara and her sister Jean into the shelter, which was rather cramped for the three of them but if they suspected a raid was imminent they would seek shelter at Bethnal Green tube station. Barbara's dad worked for the Admiralty as a civilian driver so was often away from home during air raids.

During the last week of August plans were drawn up to evacuate children from crowded cities to the open spaces of the countryside and what was hoped would be relative safety. Barbara recalled going with her sister to stay with relatives in Torquay. Her mum then moved with Barbara and Jean into a house in Torquay until she got homesick for Bethnal Green. Barbara's family lived on Old Ford Road, Bethnal Green, in an old house built in 1861 belonging, at that time, to The Crown Estate. Along with many other properties the house suffered bomb damage during the war when the roof was blown off from a nearby explosion and many of the windows were blown out.

Plans were laid down for children to be taken by their parents to a local school. On the first morning of this evacuation a curious but eerie silence blanketed the streets following the march-past of rows of children, all labelled and clutching a small bundle of possessions, together with the obligatory gas mask. Many spoke of the empty streets where once children had played in groups laughing and calling to each other. After frequently long journeys they arrived at faraway rural destinations to be met by strangers who were invited to 'choose an evacuee'. If locals had a spare room they were legally obliged to take in an evacuee. Often those who looked a little weak or unkempt would be left to the last.

Many mothers were invited to accompany their children and often this invitation was accepted. The children and their mothers would be expected to work for their hosts and many who had never been to the countryside were surprised by the different way of life. Not all adults or children adjusted easily, in fact some were never able to fit into this rural life style. Many children and their mothers returned to their homes after a short while when no enemy action seemed imminent.

Gas masks had been issued to the British population. It was an offence to not carry your gas mask, or your recently issued numbered identity card with you at all times. Children found most of this abrupt change to their young lives quite an adventure. Little children had a brightly coloured mask which was shaped to form a character and were known as *Micky Mouse Gasmasks*. Even the children's gas masks became a source of amusement. The masks were a tight fitting rubber head gear with a mixed aroma of disinfectant and rubber, but children found that you could make rude noises by exhaling sharply into them so that the clammy rubber would vibrate against their cheeks.

Ted remembered sitting with his Dad and step-mother on the day that war was declared. It was a bright sunny day, not a cloud in the sky, and he recalled leaning forward in his chair listening intently to the news on the radio. When the broadcast ended, his father, James, quietly turned towards the radio and switched it off. They all sat in silence for a few moments each lost in their own thoughts of the awful though inevitable news. Ted remembered his father's sad face and in particular his misted eyes, moist with un-shed tears, no doubt remembering the previous conflict in which so many lives had been lost including that of his dear friend and brother-in-law James Norton. Just a few minutes later sirens wailed in warning of an impending air raid and people hastened into air raid shelters – this first warning though was a false alarm set off by a friendly plane carrying French officers.

Call up papers had begun to be sent out to male 20 year olds so Ted was one of the early ones to be conscripted into the Army. He was told to report to a local office where he was given a medical and his basic details were duly noted down before he was then ordered to report to a main line station at a certain time and date. Many years later, I asked my dad (Ted) what it was like at that time and he told me how it was hard to say goodbye to your family and friends not knowing if and when you would see them again. No matter how many times he came home on leave, he always found the parting at the leave end just as difficult as the first time.

Suddenly the streets were filled with people hurrying to and from recruitment offices and departure points. Many a tearful and hasty goodbye took place behind closed doors as sons and parents, wives or girlfriends spent these last precious minutes together.

Newspaper placards daily notified the public of the latest developments, with further details in their papers. Citizens were warned to be careful: *Careless talk costs lives* – was one of the many poster warnings issued by the government.

Margaret and Bert had set up home in rented accommodation in a house owned by a Mr & Mrs Pope. Margaret's husband Bert was in the Police Reserve. Margaret remembered hearing that war had been declared and how she, her husband and neighbours all left their homes and entered the air-raid shelter when the warning sounded for the first time. They whiled away the time waiting for the 'all-clear' to sound by making the shelter as habitable as possible for future use. Air raid shelters were oddly enough not compulsory nor was evacuation of women and their children to the countryside.

Many families did not have a patch of garden in which to erect an Anderson shelter, especially in some of the built up areas of East London. James Overy and his family in Leyton and the remaining Norton family in Approach Road, Bethnal Green were lucky as they did have gardens big enough to erect one of these shelters but often families daily took the risk of being killed or maimed by bombs or falling masonry by remaining in their homes during air raids.

The daily news would include the latest instructions and advice for civilians, including the sad advice (advised, not compulsory) that dogs and other domestic animals living in London, and indeed in other towns and cities across Great Britain, should be put down. The thinking was that the War would be fought as much in this country as in Europe, it had been decided that the noise of bombs dropping and exploding all around them would terrify animals and there was also the possibility that many animals might be injured and/or left homeless. Bert, on behalf of Mr & Mrs Pope, sadly took their two dogs to the vet and had them put to sleep, returning unhappily a little later with the two empty dog collars. Not all family pets were put to sleep, many families deciding to keep their pets in spite of the risks and directives on pet food that were issued. Curiously, some people reported that dogs in particular gave them an alert – perhaps rushing down into the cellar, five or ten minutes before the air raid siren sounded.

Margaret's husband Bert and their landlord Mr Pope were both called up but until Bert was given instructions on where he was to report for training he continued to serve as a Police Reserve. One night he came home from duty complaining that his recently issued tin helmet was a tight fit and thought he would try to stretch it by forcing it down over one of his young wife's cooking dishes. Unfortunately for Bert, when he tried to remove the dish from the helmet the next day he found it was stuck fast with the rim of the dish protruding slightly from the base of the helmet! Margaret struggled to hide her mirth at her husband's predicament.

Ted was sent for basic training to Maidstone in Kent at the end of which the Army posted him to the Royal West Kent Regiment. Ted found Army life, when training, a little different to what he had imagined but, Ted being Ted, managed to cause a little strife during training routine with his quick-witted mimicry and many a pail of potatoes were peeled due to his training sergeant having 'super tuned hearing' (Ted's words).

Autumn 1940 had been glorious but the winter of 1940/41 was particularly bitter, often pipes froze and had to be gently thawed out with a candle flame. Bert was still training in the UK away from home and Margaret was invited to stay with Bert's aunt and uncle in Hatfield, their daughter Millie was the same age as Margaret so this arrangement seemed a very good idea. When Bert came home on leave, they packed up their belongings and put them into storage with relatives. Many families living away from the capital offered shelter to relations living in London, sometimes because these relations had been 'bombed out' of their homes, but often the offer was made to get them to a safer area outside of London.

James Overy and his wife Lizzie had moved in with relatives for a while as their little house in Leyton had suffered severe bomb damage. Eventually they moved into a house in Argyll Street, Stepney, where they remained for the rest of their lives.

People's lives were being disrupted on a daily basis with the advent of war. Once familiar sights such as road signs were removed and a constant flow of uniformed personnel thronged the streets. Time became very precious with the fast changing way of life and the future seemed very uncertain. Bert knew he was about to be sent overseas so once he had seen Margaret settled in with his aunt and uncle in Hatfield, he and Margaret took a train back to London to visit Bert's mother and brothers to say his goodbyes. Their return journey to Hatfield was far from peaceful though. As they boarded the train in London, the sirens began to wail out a warning of an imminent air-raid. There were troops in all the carriages so they were hurriedly placed in the guard's van. They found themselves in complete darkness and the only way they could hope to find their destination was to try to count the stations and listen for the porter shouting out the name of the station each time the train stopped. Tired, but grateful to have got through the ordeal, they eventually arrived back in Hatfield.

Ted's first depot posting, once he had joined the Royal West Kents, was in Tonbridge, Kent. He and six others were billeted in unoccupied premises in the High Street. They arrived late at night and were just glad to get to their destination, bunk down and get some sleep, but after a reasonable night's sleep they awoke to find there was no water as the pipes had frozen.

Ted went out to find water but found my mother-to-be instead. His first words to her when he spotted her leaving the house next door were not at all romantic, "Have you got any water, Ma?"

Vera, being a little nervous of all these strangers in her home town, did not speak much but pointed to an inside tap for him to fill the bucket. After this first chance meeting, and being next door neighbours, over the next few days they often met by accident. Vera was nineteen years-old when they met and he almost twenty-one. Many couples met during the War through being posted to places up and down the country and this led to large numbers of couples marrying who may never have met, but for the advent of war.

In a few weeks though, Ted was posted back to Maidstone where he was lucky enough to be transferred to the Royal Electrical & Mechanical Engineers (REME), a posting which may well have saved his life. He had been chosen for training in this unit due to his apprenticeship skills in electrical work, whereas most of his new-found friends were not so lucky and were sent to become front line infantrymen. Battalions of the Royal West Kents served in every major theatre, and were involved in a great deal of combat from Dunkirk to the final assault on Germany, from North Africa to Burma. There were several thousand casualties with this regimental organisation alone.

Ted and Vera started to write to each other but they did not meet up until Ted was transferred on to Stourbridge just outside Canterbury. Ted was by nature an optimistic and positive individual who could always find humour in many of life's daily incidents. He was not afraid of work but found some of the 'square bashing' as he termed it, rather excessive. I recall one story he told me of the 10 mile route marches that the unit would regularly undertake. It was, after all, necessary to ensure all the soldiers were fit and capable of enduring long marches over unknown and sometimes rough terrain but Ted, being a young man, did not always see it as being important to the training. He disliked pomp and found the fact that the march would start in the town with the band playing with a mustering of as many of the locals lining the streets to wave them off, a little over the top. Once they reached the end of the town and crossed the bridge over the little River Stour, the band would stop then part ranks allowing the soldiers to pass through to continue their march.

The band then returned to barracks only to meet up with the troops at the bridge at the end of the march and play them back through the town.

Ted and a few of his friends decided that no one would notice if they slipped away at the same time as the band and re-joined at the end of the march, after all they had done most of the marches. Absconding from the next planned march, all went well until they returned to barracks and lined up on the parade ground for inspection. The eagle eyed sergeant noticed that a few of the troops were not as tired or travel stained as the rest of them, neither could he recall seeing them on the march. He could not prove it of course but he kept his eye on them from then on, and they knew it, so did not try to dodge any more marches.

Whilst Ted and others were getting into shape before being sent to fight for their country, civilians at home were

Ted in the West Kent's uniform c.1940-41

preparing for war in different ways. It was a time known as the Phoney War, as many had expected an immediate bombardment from Germany and her allies. However, during the next seven months, although all the nations involved were massing armaments and making preparations to protect their citizens, no enemy offensive had commenced in Europe although fighting was taking place in other theatres, including the air and at sea.

In May 1940, Anthony Eden the War Minister, called for a new voluntary force to be set up which started life as the Local Defence Volunteers but eventually became known as 'Dad's Army'. The stipulation of recruits' fitness was that they should be capable of free movement! The LDV in Bethnal Green was based at the Town Hall but could often be seen drilling and marching around Victoria Park. The park was mainly closed to the public for the duration of the war, having been turned over to military use. Victoria Park was of great strategic importance as it was along the path the German bombers took after bombing raids on the London docks and warehouses. Anti-aircraft (Ack-Ack or AA) sites were set up in the park. Later in the war a new 'Z Battery' was installed in the park with fateful consequences (see Chapter 18).

Twice weekly, the *Hackney Gazette* would publish court cases of shops being fined for overcharging. On a more humorous note, the paper also requested its readers to stop writing to Mr A Hitler because the G.P.O. (the General Post Office as it was known then), was unable to deliver any letters to him at the present time!

Barrage balloons began to appear in the skies made of bright shiny material that sparkled in sunlight. They were anchored to the ground by guy ropes which gave off a gentle humming noise when it was breezy. When viewed from below, the groups of barrage balloons resembled shoals of whales floating on high. The balloon cables were effective at deterring low level enemy planes. Sometimes in bad weather a balloon broke free or would have to be cut free and the resultant damage to chimney pots or roofs as they careered wildly in the air was an accepted part of the price to pay for the protection they gave.

In the midst of doubt and uncertainty, life had some pleasure for the families when an engagement was announced between young Phoebe Deeks and Charles Kerridge. Phoebe vividly remembered Mrs Kerridge, her future mother-in-law, giving her a little engagement tea party. Phoebe thought that all the guests had arrived but there was a surprise in store for her. Mrs Kerridge (knowing who was outside) asked Phoebe to answer the door for her and to Phoebe's delight when she opened the door she found, on the door step, Ted and Eddy, in their army uniforms.

Later that evening, Ted and Eddy sat on a bench either side of Phoebe at the side of the fireplace watching the flames gently flicker through the coals and listening to the song *Deep Purple* on the radio. As they swayed from side to side in time with the music they started to softly sing the words. Phoebe said that, for many years after, whenever she heard the song, she would be transported back to that moment. She was 93 years old when she told me of their engagement party and, as she spoke, you could hear the delight this memory gave her. In the midst of war, happiness could still be found by civilians and moments like these would be savoured just in case it was the last time they ever saw each other. Among the many important facts that the war would teach those who lived through it was just how precious time really was.

In January 1940 rationing was introduced, no doubt from lessons learnt through the shortages and subsequent rationing that had occurred during the First World War. But no one realised at that time how long rationing would remain in force – indeed, some items were rationed for a further fourteen years.

All UK citizens were issued with a ration book; citizens were required to register themselves, their children, and family at local shops and food was issued based on a coupon system. Food was paid for but you could only obtain certain items in restricted quantity, unless of course you resorted to illegal black market supplies at an inflated price. The first items to go on ration were meat and dairy products.

The standard adult rations for a week for most of the war period were:

1lb 3 ozs of meat	538.6	grams
4 ozs bacon or ham	113.5	..
3 pints of milk	1.7	litres
2 ozs of butter	56.7	grams
2 ozs of margarine	56.7	..
2 ozs fat or lard	56.7	..
2 ozs of loose tea	56.7	..
1 egg		
2 ozs jam	56.7	grams
3 ozs of sugar	85.5	..
1 oz of cheese	28.4	..
2 lb of onions	907.2	..

People could also obtain a tin of dried egg powder in exchange for a month's egg ration. Or as an alternative to fresh milk people could use a month's coupons to obtain a tin of dried milk. Clothes were also rationed as factories were required to switch production to other products to assist the war effort. Gradually more commodities were rationed such as petrol with books of tokens being issued separately to vehicle owners.

The Ministry of Food issued posters and radio advice on self-sufficiency, with slogans such as *Dig for Victory* aimed at encouraging people to grow their own vegetables, on any patch of spare land, including bomb sites. James Overy, always a keen gardener, decided that he could grow marrows on the earth over the Anderson shelter in their little garden and so he set to work tending his little Anderson shelter vegetable patch but his wife Lizzie found the sight of the raised mound of earth topped with the yellow flowers of the marrows rather morbid as they reminded her of a grave with funeral flowers. Undeterred by his wife's comments he continued to grow many of these and other vegetables each year throughout the war. He would remind her with a grin on his face that he was 'digging for victory – just as the government directive recommended'.

People were also encouraged to save any leftover scraps of food for livestock and many people banded together to form 'pig clubs' in order to provide meat for the table. None of the Norton, Overy, Deeks or Bates families belonged to these clubs but occasionally a chicken or a rabbit would be 'given' to one of the families in payment of a good turn. James Overy came home briefly one day with a bag and said he had been given a rabbit. Lizzie and Margaret thought it would be a welcome supplement to their rations but soon changed their minds once they opened the bag and out hopped a terrified rabbit!

As the war years progressed, the Ministry of Food advertised recipes, such as cake mixture with mashed potato and carrot croquettes, to make your rations go further with home grown vegetables. A *Potato Pete Recipe Book* was printed and distributed by the Ministry, in order to encourage people into growing their own vegetables (*Dig for Victory* again). Aunt Lydie told me that many of the recipes were rather tasteless, there was even a vegetable dish named after the Minister of Food – Woolton Pie. As white flour became scarce, a new 'National' loaf was introduced to the nation's diet. You would now describe this as 'granary' bread, though the colour was not brown but grey. The population had no choice but to eat this as there were no other bread varieties available.

Posters also appeared to encourage citizens to 'Make do and Mend', resulting in many women becoming skilled in the art of letting clothes down or out for their children or altering their own clothes by adding a lace collar from an old lace curtain.

Civilians were asked to give up their aluminium pots and pans for the war effort. Many houses had small front gardens with wrought iron gates and small decorative railings. Soon those railings and others from parks and public buildings were requisitioned to be melted down for the production of armaments. Tramlines were also dug up for this purpose. When visiting Bethnal Green as a child, I was for a while puzzled by the sight of little stumps of iron protruding from a low wall at the front of houses, many railings were never restored in the post-war era.

Life went on in spite of the war and a spring wedding took place in 1940 when Phoebe Deeks married Charles Kerridge. The Norton, Overy, Bates and Deeks families gathered to witness the marriage and to celebrate with the happy couple, albeit a marriage in the midst of the extended family's Second World War.

16

Enduring the *Blitz*

On Saturday 7 September 1940 during daylight hours, the first '*Blitz*' was unleashed on East London by Germany when 375 aircraft dropped their bomb cargoes on pre-defined targets. The Luftwaffe returned that night to further ravage the East End of London and this time found the target area very easily from the fires still raging after the earlier daylight raid. Indeed the fires were so intense that the inferno could be seen from mid-way across the English Channel. It was Germany's belief that air attacks such as these would terrorise the inhabitants and thereby force the British Government to negotiate peace terms with Germany; however, as would prove to be the case from 1943 onwards with massive Allied bombing of German cities, such raids had the opposite effect on civilian morale as Londoners, East Enders in particular, kept going with the words 'we can take it', or at least this was the official line given out although many people became traumatised by the relentless bombing raids.

Between 7 and 24 September, there were continuous air raids. During this time ninety-five high explosive bombs ranging in size from 50-1,000kg together with two parachute mines and an overwhelming number of incendiary bombs rained down on Bethnal Green itself.

One of the casualties on this first day of the *Blitz* was the church where Maggie and James had married in 1913. St Matthew's church took a direct hit during the night of 7

September, leaving this formerly beautiful church roofless and in ruins. The parishioners were undaunted and services continued to be held within the open-air ruined church. A temporary church was erected after the war until it was decided in 1957 to rebuild the church, with work commencing in 1958. The church was finally re-consecrated on 15 July 1961.

Recent photographs of the interior and exterior of the re-built St Matthew's Church.

Two further casualties of the night of 7 September I feel I should mention out of many: the Columbia Road Market Building and the local library. At the start of the war, the Columbia Road Market building had been designated as a large public shelter and on this particular night a 50kg bomb was dropped overhead; its deadly destination was one of the air vents – there were many casualties and some fatalities. The Bethnal Green Library took a direct hit that night too. Eventually Bethnal Green Council opened a temporary lending library in Bethnal Green Underground Shelter, with a stock of approximately 4,000 books.

A family recollection of the bombings of the night of 11 September came from the Bates family. They had gone to bed in their flat in Guinness Buildings, Columbia Road – the grandparents in the bedroom and the rest of the family sheltering under the table. Shortly afterwards, the nightly bombing raid began with a bomb landing just outside the flats. Charlie Deeks Snr had downed a few drinks before the raid started so was convinced the Germans had hit him personally when a bottle, jarred into movement by the exploding bomb outside, fell off the table and onto his head – "They got me!" he said indignantly.

Granddad had pushed the wardrobe in front of the window before the raid started but as an additional precautionary measure, when he heard the bomb whistling through the air, he threw a blanket over his wife's head. As the raid intensified, the family decided to leave the flat for the shelter as they felt they would perhaps be safer there than under the table. They picked their way carefully down the staircase, feeling the scrunching of broken glass beneath their feet. Finally, they reached the surface shelter.

Granddad thought a nip of brandy, purchased on a trip to Boulogne the previous year, would help steady everyone's nerves, but his daughter was promptly sick when she tried the remedy.

"Look at that!" said her father in disgust. "What a waste of good brandy!"

Meanwhile, the nearby Baxendale public house on the corner of Columbia Road and Shipton Street was destroyed in the raid along with the little cottages in Baxendale Street. Phoebe's brother's funeral (Arthur) had taken place earlier that day and with typical Cockney humour upon hearing of the

Baxendale public house fate someone quipped that Arthur had taken the pub with him!

Later the following day when they left the shelter and viewed the damage, they found a huge crater where once the pub had stood. The Bates family also discovered that inside their flat the dinner service had been blown off the dresser and the wallpaper ripped from the walls. Although this account may sound humorous it was anything but and many people found the trauma of incessant raids more than they could psychologically bear.

Following the first night of bombing, there were a total of 56 consecutive nights of bombing over the coming months, more than 70 in total, night and day, with the exception of one night due to bad weather.

The *Blitz* lasted for nine long months during which London together with other major cities was pounded by the *Luftwaffe*. East London in particular was targeted because of the docks and other vital industries in the area. Each raid brought fresh carnage to once familiar landscapes. Many people witnessed sights that would remain with them for the rest of their lives as they helped search for survivors buried beneath fallen buildings.

Night after night civilians, who did not have a private shelter, would form queues, clutching babies and bundles of belongings on which to sleep, anxiously waiting to enter the safety of a public shelter. A good night's sleep became a thing of the past, only the exhaustion from lack of sleep allowed a few hours of oblivion. In spite of the propaganda giving the impression that East Enders were coping with it all, the truth of the matter was that large numbers of people were not. Many spoke of the fear of each air raid attack and dreaded the onset of night when the raids would start. No wonder so many Royal visits were made to the East End of London during the War doubtless they were made in an attempt to prevent social unrest. The Queen, after Buckingham Palace was hit by bombs whilst she was there, famously said, "At last I can look the East Enders in the face." Those who did not have shelters or who were determined to stand up to the bombardment would seek shelter under furniture, beneath stairs, in a cupboard or down in a cellar (if they had one) anything that could accommodate them and give a sense of security.

Margaret's husband Bert was given instructions to report for duty with the Royal Air Force at Uxbridge. They recalled how unreal life seemed at that time. Margaret and her peers were expected to carry personal papers, gas mask and identity cards with them at all times but often items of shopping would be tucked into the bag and occasionally small items could get forgotten and left in the bag for weeks, unless it was a perishable item which would make itself known by its decomposing odour.

Each day would bring a further change to the once familiar landscape as the bombs reshaped their local area. Once a bombing raid was over local people would stoically gather to start to clean up the debris into neat piles by the side of the roads, as if their actions would bring some normality to the situation.

Some nights the bombing was very intense and many of the family could recall that if a bomb fell near to their home, the building would often shake violently. Out in the streets, shrapnel from the bombs would viciously stab and bounce in a macabre dance along its deadly path until spent or until some unfortunate person became its final destination. Once a bomb fell, the explosion would not only send up clouds of dust from the buildings being torn apart but a great vacuum of air would often tear clothes from the backs of people nearby. Frequently, people would describe the ensuing suction as feeling as if their eyes were being sucked from their sockets. Often, after raids as people emerged from shelters they would come face to face with victims' bodies, some found with their limbs torn from their torsos, in some cases decapitated bodies would be discovered as rescuers frantically tore into the wreckage seeking survivors.

Shops and offices closed early to allow their staff to gain the safety of shelter before the night raids commenced. Next morning people would resurface to find the air filled with the acrid smell of brick dust and smoke. Many families who lost their homes in raids did not have family to seek shelter with and were cared for in improvised Rest Centres, staffed by volunteers. Often in deep shock and suffering from exhaustion, the homeless would stay in these centres for weeks on end until accommodation could be found for them.

Together with the local council, which did not have sufficient dwelling stock within the borough, and was struggling to meet the demand for accommodation from those made homeless, the local Public Assistance Committee was tasked with the unenviable responsibility of housing the homeless as they were responsible for the whole of Greater London and therefore could draw on any surplus resources around the perimeter of Central London. Not all were permanently homeless. Some victims would only need temporary shelter if their home was, for example, near an unexploded bomb, but many homes were lost or severely damaged in the bombing raids leaving large numbers of families desperately seeking assistance.

James Overy had made their Anderson Shelter as comfortable as possible but he and Margaret, who often stayed with her parents while Bert was away training, frequently chose to stand in the garden to watch the never ending flashes and sparks in the sky from gunfire or flares in the distance. They always kept within easy reach of the shelter entrance though, just in case. At one point an old lady, a friend of Lizzie's, stayed with them for a couple of months, presumably because she herself had been bombed out of her home. The lady was known as a sweet kindly soul. Margaret was charged with making sure the old lady got into the shelter when the warning siren sounded. Margaret and her dad James often laughed at Lizzie's attempts at conversation with the dear old lady, who was partially deaf, as Lizzie's voice moved up the scale and grew louder and louder as she tried desperately to compete with the noise of the bombs falling and exploding and, if they looked in the shelter sometimes, they would see a red-faced Lizzie almost at the point of exhaustion from the effort.

Vera recalled watching from where she lived in Tonbridge, Kent (some thirty-five miles from London), a large bright fiery glow light up the sky over the East End of London night after nightfall. Sometimes she would watch alone but at times her father would stand with her sadly staring at this evil glow staining the night sky.

At the start of World War Two many people had voiced, as in the First World War, the optimistic wish that, "It will be all over by Christmas." Now, as they moved towards the second Christmas of the war, people were mindful that the children would need some normality in their young lives and the celebration of Christmas, at this difficult time, would hopefully give this to the children. None-the-less, many spent the festive season in Anderson shelters, or in underground stations, decorated of course with paper chains and perhaps a small Christmas tree or some holly. Mothers and fathers would hang little stockings up for the children. As food was not as yet fully rationed but with rationing due to start in the New Year, many families decided to try to make Christmas as normal as possible – given the blackout restrictions that impacted on the usual festive sights. Gifts that wartime Christmas tended to be of a practical nature – for adults perhaps gardening tools or gas mask cases in Rexine or leather;

for children, miniature RAF or Red Cross uniforms were very popular. For many adults that second wartime Christmas was also a time to sadly reflect on life in the war and those loved ones already lost in the Blitz as well as wondering how many more family members and friends they would lose in the coming months and years...

17

The Early Years of World War Two

Whilst the Second World War was being fought at home and abroad, a semblance of life in Bethnal Green, as in the rest of Britain, continued for civilians. Ted who was now effectively courting Vera would visit her in Kent and his family in London as often as he was able to when granted weekend passes or periods of leave. One visit in 1941 was to see his Uncle Ted and Aunt Lydie and their daughter Susie. Ted was very fond of his relatives and would take little gifts whenever he could. He knew that young Susie would not experience the variety of fruit he had as a boy, indeed some fruits such as bananas ('specky' or otherwise) were never seen during the war. Oranges would only occasionally appear but were clearly marked 'for children only', so when Ted managed to get an unheard of luxury in the form of a pomegranate, he decided he would give this to his little cousin.

Susie remembered for the rest of her life the valuable lesson of sharing that he taught her on this visit. Ted, or Teddy as Susie had named him, arrived unexpectedly early one afternoon. Susie was playing with her little friend but they rushed to greet Ted as they were always thrilled by his visits. After a while, Ted pulled from his pocket the lovely large pomegranate and held it out for the girls to admire before handing it to a delighted Susie. However, her smile faded a little when Ted said that she must share the fruit with her friend. Susie, probably like any child given something precious, momentarily wished her friend had not come round to play that day so she could have had the fruit all to herself. Ted, having been a child himself once, could read her thoughts; he told her to share the fruit fairly, one child should cut it in two and the other should have first choice. Susie thought for a moment then, with a willingness to please Teddy, and to make sure she got a full half, carefully cut the fruit *exactly* in two halves rather than cut it into two unequal pieces.

Eddie, Ted's cousin, had also been called up by 1940 and was stationed in Cowdenbeath in Scotland. Out with friends one night, an attractive strawberry-blonde young lady caught his eye but he did not approach her as he thought the man with

Ted and Eddie were very close friends as well as being cousins and decided to have their photo taken in their army uniforms; Ted has no insignia but Eddie appears be in the RASC.

her was her boyfriend. Later he was introduced to the 'boyfriend', John, and his *sister* Janet. Once he found out John was her brother, he asked Janet out and their romance blossomed. Janet and her sisters eventually came south of the border to live with another aunt in Streatham.

Many war-time romances were born from the necessity of forces personnel being stationed up and down the country and some romances would go on to become lifelong partnerships which would usually, for the wife, mean a change of home town to one many miles away from where she had grown up.

When the first bombs were dropped over London, a lack of adequate shelters meant many people would try to seek shelter in underground stations dotted beneath London streets. At first the government ordered stations to be locked against the public as they felt that people would develop a 'deep shelter' mentality and refuse to surface to carry on with their essential work during the daytime but eventually they had to concede and began supplying bunk beds and toilets to make the shelters a little more habitable. To gain access to a station, people would usually need a 'station ticket' which could be obtained in advance for the duration of the war and would be clearly marked 'for shelter use only' with a disclaimer about entering at your own risk.

The government also instigated station rules. Before 7:30pm people had to stay behind a line drawn eight feet from the edge of the platform. From 7:30pm -10:30pm they could take up positions within four feet of the platform edge but once the trains stopped running, the electricity to the rails would be turned off and the lights would dim at which point shelterers could make use of the entire width of the platform and in some cases people were known to sleep between the tracks until they were called to move before the power was switched back on in the early hours of the morning. These rules did not apply to Bethnal Green station as the station was only partially built. Nevertheless, the station was as heavily relied upon by the local population as were other completed or long standing stations in the metropolis.

The government had provided purpose-built public shelters but these were often unsuitable. Many were unable to withstand close bomb blasts, resulting in the brick-built sides collapsing and the concrete roof crushing those unfortunate enough to be sheltering within at the time. There were two basic types: a walled block with a four inch concrete roof, prone to near-miss collapses, and an elongated half-egg curved shelter of entirely reinforced concrete, partly buried beneath the ground with the removed soil piled on top, which only a direct hit would damage. Both could hold a hundred or more people and were equipped with stoves and bunk beds.

If raids were taking place on a continuous basis then people would seek shelter even before an air raid warning sounded. People would try to stake a claim to a patch of underground station platform for their families as early as 11:30am with father joining them after work if he was not on fire-watching duty. Not everyone found comfort in the depths of the underground shelter. Some found the experience terrifying as they sat in the shelter listening to the horrific sound of the bombs landing and exploding above them. Witnesses speak of being able to sense, even smell, the fear felt by those within the shelters as they waited helplessly for the raid to end.

Adults would try to make the experience as normal as possible for the children in all the types of shelter even though conditions were not always very sanitary. Toilet facilities in fact were extremely primitive and with little or no privacy, personal hygiene such as washing and changing clothes was often compromised. Sleeping was difficult with so many people sheltering in such a confined space and the night hours would be peppered with the sounds of babies crying, people snoring, coughing and sneezing as well as necessary toilet trips with the attendant aromas drifting through the crowds.

Aunt Lydie, her daughter Susie and her niece Lydia with her little son George could often be found sheltering in Bethnal Green Station during heavy bombing raids. Aunt Lydie recalled the scramble into the shelter and the fear growing by the hour as the planes droned overhead dropping their deadly cargoes. Sometimes the platform shook with the violence of the explosion if a bomb landed directly overhead. There was always a fear of some kind of disastrous hit. These fears were fully justified but the disaster, in the end, would take a very different form.

During one of these nights sheltering as they sat listening to the devastation above them, aunt and niece made a pact just in case one of them should not survive; each woman agreed they would care for the other's child. Obviously, both women did have husbands but the children were too young to be left without care. Fortunately, neither woman was called upon to fulfil their pledge. I am sure this was a common pact amongst friends and relatives during these desperate times and I can still see, in my mind's eye, Aunt Lydie relating this episode to me as if it were yesterday.

The *Luftwaffe* continued its bombing of East London on a regular basis. On the night of 19 March 1941, there had been bombing in the vicinity of Approach Road, Bethnal Green with further bombing raids being carried out during early April but, during the nights of 19 and 20 April, Approach Road was very heavily bombed. At the junction of Bishops Way and Approach Road, the London Chest Hospital on the opposite side of the road took a direct hit and was severely

Recent photographs of Approach Road with the London Chest Hospital.
The Approach Tavern (over) (see p 94 for an earlier photo) and 49 Approach
Road (below). The side wall of 49 Approach Road was partially demolished
in the raid if you visit the house today you can see by the line of different
bricks where the wall was torn down.

damaged and many of the nearby houses in Approach Road were partially demolished by the explosion. Further down Approach Road the family home was shaken violently when a high explosive bomb fell outside the Approach Tavern public house on the opposite corner, the blast being so great that it partially demolished the pub and left a large crater in the road. By the morning of 21 April, Approach Road was a scene of utter devastation and the Congregational Chapel near the entrance to Victoria Park in Approach Road lay in ruins.

During this same bombing raid, an incendiary device fell on the family home badly damaging the side wall and roof. Following these raids Lydia, George and little George and Lydie, Ted and Susie were forced to leave 49 Approach Road as the house, for the time being, was no longer habitable, but the local council was able to give them temporary accommodation. Lydie and her family were rehoused in Horatio House, Bethnal Green but Lydia and her family were rehoused in a Nissen hut elsewhere in Bethnal Green.

During a bombing raid on the night of 10/11 May, 1941, Columbia Buildings was also heavily bombed. Often after bombing raids people's salvaged belongings would be piled up outside where they had once lived, nothing more than a sad reminder of what had once been home – no matter how humble. Sadly, many belongings were looted by unscrupulous people; often these looters came from outside the area. I think this must have been one of the worst wartime crimes. On the other side of the coin, Civil Defence workers often risked their lives in order to help those buried within shattered buildings, many of these workers sustaining injuries or even losing their own lives trying to save others.

To give an example of the damage sustained by Bethnal Green, from 7 October 1940 to 6 June 1941, in Bethnal Green North, 30 high-explosive bombs and 3 parachute mines were dropped. In Bethnal Green South, there were 34 high-explosive bombs and 2 parachute mines – these latter being huge devices set on a time fuse. For a small area this was a large cache of explosives. There was more before and after for the above does not include the bombs dropped from 7 September with the onset of the *Blitz* nor any bombs, V1/V2 rockets, or incendiary devices targeted on Bethnal Green after 6 June 1941 to the end of the war.

Meanwhile, Vera and Ted would write and visit each other whenever Ted was able to get some leave. In late 1941 Ted invited Vera to London for the weekend to meet his family. Ted had known Vera's family since he had met her in 1940 but this was the first time he had introduced her to his family. It was also the first time Vera had been to London and she was shocked to see the devastation wrought by the frequent bombing raids, whole areas being laid waste where once thriving communities had lived and worked. Ted pointed out to her places of interest as they walked from the tube station to his home but some of these were by now in a ruinous state.

The progression of romances during the war was different for many couples not only because of the country being on a war footing, but because many couples did not both live locally, so meeting the families was more of a formal greeting.

Naturally Ted and his family told various relatives and friends that he was bringing Vera home for the first time and, being a close family, as many as possible wanted to meet her. Uncle Ted, a woodcarver during the week, helped out part-time at the weekends in a local pub and Ted took Vera along to meet his uncle who was busy behind the bar most of the time but during a lull in the orders he was able to have a conversation with the young couple and made Vera feel very welcome, as did his wife and daughter when they met later. Here began a lifelong friendship between Aunt Lydie and Vera.

Vera recalled meeting young Susie for the first time who smiled and chatted to her cousin's girlfriend as did cousin Lydia and her little baby George that weekend. Ted put Vera back on the train at London Bridge that Sunday evening and then returned to his army barracks, thinking back on what a lovely weekend it had been – in spite of the war!

The next time Vera came to London, Ted's cousin, Eddy, was on leave and met Vera for the first time. He also introduced his girlfriend, Janet, to Vera and from then on throughout the war the four of them corresponded regularly. A lifetime friendship was founded between four young people. Many friendships such as these were forged during the war. Frequently, when Vera came to London to visit Ted and his family for the weekend, the bombing raids would start shortly after dark and Vera would witness at first hand the frequent and devastating bombing that the East London was subjected to.

Lizzie had been badly frightened by the bombing of their house in Leyton and, as a consequence, as soon as the sirens sounded she would rouse the occupants and hurry them out of the house and into the Anderson shelter. Vera remembered one night the air raid sirens sounding their warnings on several occasions, and each time the warning sounded, they all got out of bed and went down to the shelter; once the 'all clear' sounded they returned to their beds. On the last occasion the warning sounded that night, Vera thought she would rather take her chances but Lizzie was adamant. So Vera, bleary eyed, wearily trudged off with the rest of the family to the shelter. It must have been very hard living in the area at this time, a prime and frequent target of the *Luftwaffe* while trying to maintain some semblance of normality in day to day life.

As rationing became more stringent, it was becoming increasingly difficult to get some of the basic foodstuffs – even with your coupons. There were alternatives to rationing, if you had the facilities - your own chickens and resulting eggs, perhaps rabbits for the pot – and of course there was a flourishing black-market but not everyone could afford the prices. Vera, who was in the Land Army by 1941, was given the opportunity to take any cracked eggs she found on the poultry farm where she worked. She knew that Ted's family were often short of eggs so would send some of these 'surplus' eggs up to London via the brewery delivery lorry when it called at the public house near-by. The landlord and her father were old friends, which made it easier to ask the favour to pass on these precious commodities. Luckily for Vera no one questioned this occasional convoy of eggs. She was, I am sure, not the only person trying to help others – doing her bit for the war effort, you might say, and Ted's family must have been very grateful.

Not only did the civilian population suffer the bombings, food rationing, sleep deprivation as well as worry about those family members at sea or fighting abroad – but significant numbers of 'civilians' were also required to carry out fire-watching duties after they had completed their day's work. James Overy was detailed to fire-watch at Charrington the Brewery in Mile End where he still worked. Many were required to watch for fires at buildings in the vicinity of where they lived. The idea was to phone in to HQ if their building was hit and start then to fight the fire!

Margaret was appointed to fire-watch. Perhaps the word 'training' was rather a misnomer for the somewhat sketchy induction to fire-watching that Margaret remembered receiving. She was part of a group of young women who had been enlisted for the role and they were told to meet the ARP Warden on an area of waste ground for training at an appointed day and time. An army hut had been erected on waste ground and the women were divided into groups of three, one person to man (or, should I say, woman) the stirrup pump, one to fill the buckets that the pump drew the water from and the third person to direct the hose from the stirrup pump into the flames. The first day of training consisted of crawling towards the hut which was by now smoke-filled for training purposes. One young lady arrived for training wearing a fur coat! Doubtless she thought she might be exempted due to her expensive attire but unsurprisingly she was still required to crawl on the ground the same as the other trainees. Margaret's first fire-watching post was a wooden shed behind some rows of bombed-out houses. Before the war, the shed had been used to store mussels and still smelt of salty crustations long after the last mussel had been evicted. Her friends all thought it highly amusing that she had to stand in the doorway of a disused mussel shed as her part of the war effort.

The ARP Wardens were tasked with ensuring that civilians were trained to deal with putting out fires and, where necessary, rescuing injured people from burning or fire damaged premises – a dangerous task, fraught with the possibility of falling debris from the stricken building and the air thick with dust and grime from masonry torn apart in the explosions leaving a thick man-made fog that limited visibility in the search for both survivors and bodies. On an even more sombre note, many victims on these occasions, as well as their rescuers were traumatised by what they witnessed. There was no counselling at that time, everyone had to get through experiences as best they could. This physical and mental stress was particularly evident following the tragic local catastrophe in March 1943 (covered in detail in Chapter 18).

Another Christmas came and went and still the war continued, with no end in sight. Ted was posted up and down Great Britain often for short periods, wherever he was needed and, if that posting was far away, then contact with loved ones would be restricted to letter writing, as it was for many servicemen and women especially those posted overseas. The sending and receiving of letters was a joy for both parties, particularly for the recipients as they knew that their loved ones were safe – at least up until when the letter had been penned and posted.

Vera received a letter one day from Ted inviting her to visit him in Dover, his latest posting. Plans were laid to meet at Dover railway station and spend a few precious hours together. Vera caught the train to Dover and spent the journey looking forward to seeing her boyfriend again but little did she know how brief a sight of him she would get.

She recalled that it was a beautiful bright day as the train drew slowly into Dover station. Vera stood up, straightened her hat, smoothed her coat then opened the carriage door and stepped onto the platform. As she looked up, out of the corner of her eye she saw an army uniformed person running on the bridge over the platform as if his life depended upon it and, to her alarm, realised it was Ted!

He almost jumped the last few steps down off the bridge as he rushed towards Vera. Breathlessly, he explained that suddenly all leave had been cancelled and he had, unbeknown to his sergeant, sneaked out of the barracks to come and tell her. He was sorry but she would have to get the next train back. He hurried her over the bridge to the other platform just as the train bound for Tonbridge was pulling in. One hug and a kiss and Ted put her on the train then speedily returned to barracks before he was noticed as being AWOL (absent without leave). The sudden cancellation of leave was a frequent occurrence for many servicemen and women.

Another time Vera visited Ted in Dover. They were able to spend a whole day together walking along the cliffs on a clear cloudless day, with a chill in the air as autumn days had arrived. They stopped for a while and sat on a bench holding hands looking out to sea as they chatted about general everyday matters, then their conversation inevitably turned to how long the war would last. The following day, the bench was hit by a stray bomb and blown to pieces! Unsurprisingly, they did not plan any further meetings in Dover.

During the war the people of Bethnal Green, as in other parts of the country, were encouraged to partake in fundraising activities to help the war effort. During 1942, one such event was *Warship Week*. This was an incentive by the British National Savings Campaign asking communities to adopt a warship by raising funds to help pay the cost of building a ship. Local schools and churches would be encouraged to participate by sending letters and small gifts of items such as gloves and socks to crew members. Each town or borough, depending on the population size of the area, would be allocated a ship. Bethnal Green's Town Hall proudly displayed across the front of the building its poster advertising the event. *The Warship Week* was 'launched' by the Mayor, Councillor J.J Edwards, his speech being quoted in the *Hackney Gazette* edition of 20 March 1942:

> *I am not asking you to give but to lend. Our target is £250,000 which some might think rather ambitious for a small borough containing so many working-class people, who in these days of rising prices and heavy taxation find it difficult to make both ends meet; but I am certain that, with that little extra effort on the part of all, our target can be obtained, and possibly exceeded.*

I am proud to say that the people of Bethnal Green not only met the target but excelled in their efforts, raising a total of £340,481. The warship adopted was an anti-submarine sloop HMS *Crane*. The sloop had a distinguished career and her battle honours include:

BISCAY 1943 - SICILY 1943 - ATLANTIC 1943-44 - NORMANDY 1944 - ENGLISH CHANNEL 1944 - OKINAWA 1945 - KOREA 1952-53

HMS *Crane* was broken up in 1965.

To raise the well-spent money, the borough held a week of events, including a procession through the streets of Bethnal Green starting at Victoria Park and finishing at Bethnal Green Gardens. Amongst other fund-raising entertainments on offer that week were concerts organised with the RAF Band playing at Arnold Circus one day and the Royal Horse Guards Band performing outside the public baths in Old Ford Road on another day. Another and somewhat comic opening to an event, as reported in the *Hackney Gazette* on 25 March 1942, was a swimming gala in which the mayor, who was opening the gala, good naturedly took part in a mock rescue episode when he divested himself of several waistcoats to reveal a bathing dress of unique design and colour before diving into the pool wearing a cocked hat to rescue a man who had fallen in only to be rescued by the man he was supposed to be trying to save.

Luckily the Town Hall did not take any direct hits as it was crucially the control room of essential services during the war. It was manned by approximately 175 volunteers, mainly council clerical staff and councillors with an additional 18 full-time paid personnel but as the war years progressed the acute shortage of manpower led to women full-time Council staff being taken on as volunteers.

Bethnal Green Borough Council was still able to provide other services for its community: two ambulance stations each with a maximum of 12 vehicles manned by 24 personnel. A Citizen's Advice Bureau operated from St Margaret's House, Old Ford Road, E2 giving valuable help and advice to the local population. In addition the council supported directly or indirectly a range of emergency services.

Following the introduction of the Compulsory Fire Guard Order of 1941-1942, the number of voluntary fire guards was doubled from 3,000 to 6,000 (Margaret was one of them). There was a messenger service which had its headquarters at St Peter's School, from where an officer-in-charge and his deputy directed 80-100 boys in various civil defence duties. Before this service was set up, these duties had been carried out by the Scouts.

The Womens Voluntary Services (WVS), based at 43 Roman Road, were invaluable in providing volunteers for a wide range of duties but their principal activities were connected with re-clothing centres, rest centres, mobile canteens and evacuation. One of the canteens they helped to run was located at the *Museum of Childhood in Bethnal Green.* As a 'museum' it was closed to the public during the war, becoming instead a *British Restaurant* to feed the public (2,160 were established across the UK). These were canteens which gave a full meal during the day at a very good rate. Eating out was popular with people as the *British Restaurant* food was 'off-ration'. Local councils ran the *British*

Restaurants, and the idea had developed from the original *London County Council Londoner's Meals Service* started in 1940 to feed people bombed out of their homes. Vera recalled a visit to the museum for a meal with Ted's family, and remembers the food being really good and how nice it was to go out and have an affordable family meal.

18

The Bethnal Green Tube Disaster

Although many terrible events took place during World War Two, one event during this period stands out in the history of Bethnal Green and I have therefore devoted a separate chapter to this disaster purely out of respect for those who tragically lost relatives and friends that night.

During the early part of 1943, a terrible accident occurred which for many many years remained hidden from the general public's knowledge. Only those who lived or worked locally knew of this tragedy: 173 people died in the worst civilian calamity in Britain during World War Two and even today it still the worst civilian death toll to have occurred in this country.

The press were ordered by the government not to report precisely what had happened as it was felt the story could badly affect public morale. Instead, official sources reported there had been a crush at a tube shelter but did not give the exact location. No bombs fell during the incident and all the casualties were the result of a series of tragic circumstances.

Sadly, it has since come to light that there was a government cover-up. Bethnal Green Borough Council had as early as 1941 written to the Government on three separate occasions to request permission to alter the single entrance to the station and so make the entrance safer; on each occasion the government refused permission. The Borough Engineer of

Bethnal Green also wrote a strongly worded letter voicing the council's concerns and explaining why the entrance to the station needed to have a longer lead-in rather than just going through the dark doorway and straight down 19 steps; he also said they needed fixed hand-rails, a more strongly built entrance and safer steps with white markings on the edge of each step as well as a cover to prevent the steps becoming wet and slippery, particularly as there had already been reports of people falling on the uneven and at times 'slippery steps'. He concluded that a proper light needed to be installed as well. At the time Bethnal Green Borough Council wrote and requested these changes, the cost would have been no more than £88.00 (£3,612 at today's value) a very small sum indeed compared to the great loss of life and the immense psychological as well as physical scarring that was suffered by many of the individuals who survived.

Many underground stations were used as public air-raid shelters by local people and the partially constructed Bethnal Green Underground Station, (one of the few deep-level stations) was heavily relied upon, being in such a densely populated area with little room for individual shelters. The government had provided the station (as an emergency shelter) with 5,000 bunks but at times it was able to shelter up to 7,000 civilians; the station had facilities such as a lending library, a medical treatment room, a small entertainment theatre and a canteen providing drinks and light refreshments. Toilets, in the form of buckets, were provided for people to relieve themselves but many chose to avoid using these if possible. As the train tracks had not been laid, a row of bunks either side of the train tunnels was put in place. The air was stale from lack of movement and often smelt of body odour from so many people sheltering cheek by jowl.

However, people often preferred to shelter in the 'underground' in spite of the lack of proper sanitary conditions, rather than spend night after night in the cramped Anderson or Morrison shelters, even if they had such a shelter of their own. People perhaps felt safer in the company of many others, especially in a much deeper refuge.

Although the *Blitz*, the prolonged bombing campaign of varying intensity, had largely ended by May 1941. Air raid sirens heralding bombing raids were still a frequent occurrence. However, with the raids lessening, people began to relax a little and stay at home rather than travel to the tube air-raid shelter each evening. If British bombers attacked Berlin or other major German cities, then Germany would typically try to retaliate with a deliberately heavier 'bombing raid' on London or other major British cities, and all too often the East End was severely hit. Local civilians were aware of this pattern and would ready themselves once they had news of a raid on Germany. The Luftwaffe had recently stopped using their slower, medium-bomber formations replacing them with lighter, smaller groups, using their fastest planes – a hit and run tactic – giving civilians less time to seek shelter once an air raid warning sounded. But still deadly.

On 3 March 1943 there was an air raid warning at 8:17 pm – by then approximately 500 people had already settled into the Bethnal Green Station shelter for the night. At the sound of the warning siren, others started to make their way to the shelter including those in nearby pubs and cinemas alerted by messages flashed onto the screens. Local people were alert and ready for reprisal raids as Britain had heavily bombed Berlin only two nights before. Suddenly, a nearby radio-controlled searchlight came on, indicating an aircraft had been detected; people stopped for a split second to look up and then began to run across Victoria Park Square to reach the safety of the shelter entrance.

There was a wooden hoarding and a narrow entrance to the station with just a small twenty-five watt light bulb. Usually there would have been a policeman or warden on duty at the door but there was no one that night as he had been called away on another matter. Due to a lessening of manpower since 1942 as more and more men had been enlisted into the forces, women and men in reserved occupations were drafted into

Mobile Z Battery c. 1943

civil defence posts but there was still a shortage of people to fill these vital positions.

It had been raining earlier in the day leaving the steps slippery but people knew where they were going because they had been there many times before. There were rope handrails at each side of the stairs but significantly there was no central stair rail. Everything appeared normal and orderly as up to

1,500 people negotiated the station steps safely down to the station shelter.

The air-raid siren had stopped but people continued to descend in an orderly fashion. Suddenly, at 8:27pm, the antiaircraft rocket batteries (known as 'Z batteries') in Victoria Park fired off 60 rockets at the supposed aircraft above. It was a new, unfamiliar battery of 'guns' and no one had heard the sound of its fire before, later described in a report as being 'a roar then a swish with a blinding orange flash' – a fearsome weapon and one that would strike terror into anyone nearby, indeed it apparently sounded very similar to a bomb falling from the sky. Just at that moment, three buses full of people arrived at the number eight bus stop (bus drivers had been given instructions that in the event of an aid raid warning they were to drive to the nearest shelter) and, above the noise, somebody shouted in fear, *'There's bombs! There's bombs! There's bombs! They're bombing us!'*

People continued, as they had done many times before, to descend the stairs quickly to reach the safety of the station depths, but the sheer volume of people at the entrance to the ill-lit tube shelter made visibility in the dark, dimly lit stairwell impossible. The first to fall was a young woman carrying a small child and her bundle (a pillow and blankets) – she may well have slipped on a wet patch on the stairs from the earlier rain. As she was falling she pulled an elderly man over and he fell on top of her. Within seconds, hundreds of people fell as – unaware of the tragedy unfolding on the steps below – civilians continued to push forward in a desperate attempt to reach safety.

With more people descending the stairs, the fallen were unable to get to their feet, causing a lethal human domino chain, each person instinctively putting their arms out in front of them to cushion their fall but instead they became hopelessly entangled with each other – arms locked together and legs trapped as they fell. Over 300 people were crushed together on the stairs. The rush of people separated children from their parents as they were pushed along on a tide of terror with people falling from above onto the mass of bodies below. Children were heard screaming for their mothers and fathers with many acts of bravery spoken of later as adults, without fear for their own personal safety, tried to help children and the elderly by plucking them from the suffocating mass of bodies that they were partially buried beneath. One young boy remembered being pulled out from the writhing throng of struggling bodies on the stairs by a warden. "You go downstairs and say nothing of what has happened here!" ordered the grim faced warden. Some of the survivors of that night were disfigured by footprints from the boots of their rescuers as they tried desperately to step over and pull the living out from the tangled mass of humanity. My cousin Gloria had a school friend, Sheila Hum, whose mother's arm carried such an imprint. One off-duty policeman, Thomas Penn, who was passing by at the time, managed to rescue the youngest survivor, a six-month old baby girl from the crush. He had spotted the mother holding up her baby over her head and asked for the baby to be passed to him but he was unable to reach the baby's mother who died in the crush.

At approximately 9pm, three people were heard walking along the tunnel – a policeman, an air raid warden and a fireman who had climbed down the shaft at Carpenters Square next to Bancroft Road. People were getting anxious as some of their friends and relatives had not arrived and as they could hear the measured tread of footsteps drawing nearer and nearer they began to whisper amongst themselves, "…why had these officials come through the tunnel?" However, the officials were well aware that there were 1,500 people in the shelter at the time and if they had given the reason, many more lives would undoubtedly have been lost in the ensuing panic, so they said nothing. By 10:30pm all had quietened down as people went to bed.

Margaret often passed Bethnal Green Tube Station (my cousin Sheila remembers her mother telling her of the shock she felt when she turned the corner, coming face to face with rows of white draped bodies lying on the ground) but she did not know at that time the real reason for all of these fatalities, nor that two of her work colleagues were among the dead. Just after midnight all the bodies had been removed and survivors had been taken to local hospitals – but no one sheltering in the station that night was allowed to leave as the authorities were understandably keen to avoid any additional incidents. People began to come out of the station at about 6am the next day and as they ascended the stairs they were met by piles of shoes and, surprisingly, found that the steps had been freshly washed down.

The next morning, Susie remembered waiting for her best friend to call for her and walk to school as they did every day but her friend never arrived, so Susie set off to walk to school alone that day. She noticed that people on the route were crying and naturally assumed that a bomb must have exploded nearby.

That morning at local schools, and those in the surrounding areas, there were many children missing from the classrooms. The teacher in Susie's classroom quietly called the register, which would have been a valuable aid in confirming those missing. Children were frightened and began to cry as they sensed something terrible had happened.

People with missing relatives had begun late that night the grim search of the hospitals hoping against hope to find their relatives safe and sound but sadly, in many cases, this was not to be. These desperate relatives travelled to The Bethnal Green Hospital, The Hackney Road Children's Hospital, The London

Chest Hospital, The German Hospital, The London Hospital, The Northern Hospital and the Mildmay Mission Hospital. The staff at the hospitals were only warned that an incident had taken place and to expect many casualties but when they arrived they found many of the victims beyond help, dead upon arrival. Puzzlingly for the staff, the bodies were noticeably wet with skin tinged a light mauve colour.

Many frantic people were unable to find their relatives and were redirected to temporary mortuaries where large numbers of bodies had been lain out awaiting identification; seeing row upon row of these lifeless, shrouded bodies brought home to the relatives the realisation that there had been an immense tragedy. Some, searching for loved-ones, were only able to identify them by known items of clothing as many of the features of the deceased were unrecognisable having been horrifically mutilated by the crush of bodies. One 14 year old girl lost her mother that night and with her older brother in the Merchant Navy and her older sister in the Air Force she had to try to live on in the family home by herself. Her brother who had been home on leave that fateful night went out searching for their mother but it was only her clothing that identified her body. Out of the total of 173 fatalities, 62 were children. A further 62 casualties were hospitalised but many who were able to walk away did so and lived as best they could with the memory of the horror of the events of that night for the rest of their lives. Ironically, among those who survived was the baby of the woman who had fallen first but sadly she died.

Aunt Lydie was terribly distressed to hear of the tragedy, though only part of the story had begun to seep out into the local neighbourhood. She anxiously waited for her daughter Susie to arrive home just after 4 o'clock and tried to reassure Susie that her little friend would surely be back at school tomorrow but tragically Susie's little friend, who had shared the pomegranate Ted had given them, was one of the children who had died in that terrible disaster.

Marie Stephens was visiting her aunt on the evening of the tragedy when a neighbour called in with the awful news that she had just visited a local hospital and seen the corridors lined with bodies even though there had not been an air raid.

Aunt Lydie asked her sister Lottie, who had moved to Buckinghamshire, if Susie could go to stay with her for a few days while the funerals took place. Lottie came to fetch her niece and tried, as much as possible, to keep her niece's mind on happier matters during those terribly sad days.

Aunt Lydie recalled seeing row upon row of little white coffins travelling slowly down the road towards the cemetery and feeling an overwhelming sadness at so many lives lost but at the same time so grateful that her dear daughter Susie had not been one of the victims. Not all the victims were buried locally as many of those that sought shelter that fateful night had travelled to Bethnal Green by the buses that had abruptly halted their journey at the Number 8 bus stop.

If you go to Bethnal Green Tube Station today, you will see a plaque in memory of this terrible tragedy and, in the nearby Bethnal Green Gardens you can see the *Stairway to Heaven Memorial* which is currently under construction. The stories on this 'partially' completed memorial are both poignant and unbelievably sad but give a small glimpse of the human cost this tragic accident dealt to so many. The final section to complete the stairway will be a canopy with 173 circles allowing light down from above as if the souls of those lost shine down from Heaven – a fitting reminder of a tragedy that should never have happened nor be forgotten. It has taken 70 years for a proper memorial to be built in memory of those innocent lives lost.

A Government Enquiry dated 3 April 1943, was held but its findings were not published in full. In fact the detailed evidence given at the Enquiry was kept locked away until 2004 – it was said originally to do so would avoid adverse enemy propaganda and prevent a loss of morale among the citizens of this country, but Lord Haw Haw[6] had broadcast details on the radio only two days after the accident. How had the truth got out to the enemy? Point 38 of the report states that:-

Before going on to deal with the rain and contributory causes of the disaster I should like at this point to deal with two specific allegations which have received some publicity, and which are without any foundation whatsoever. Each may be dismissed with a very few words:-

(a)   that this was panic induced by Fascists or criminal persons for nefarious purposes. There were some deaths among men with criminal records. They and their relatives are as much entitled to sympathy as any of the other victims. This story had some local, and I hope limited, circulation. It is an absurdity.

(b)   that there was a Jewish panic. This canard had a much wider circulation and was, I understand, endorsed by the broadcast utterances of a renegade traitor from Germany. Not only is it without foundation, it is

---

[6] William Joyce was a traitor, hanged 3 January 1945 for treason. *Lord Haw-Haw* was a nickname given to him. He broadcast propaganda from Germany beginning with "Jairmany calling, Jairmany calling", was spoken in an unintentionally comic upper-class accent. Ironically he was listened to avidly as if a comic because his claims were ridiculous. Unfortunately the laughter faded when he was shown to be right on occasion – such as the sinking of HMS *Hood*. On the other hand he 'sank' HMS *Ark Royal* several times.

demonstrably false. The Jewish attendance at this shelter was, and is, so small as to constitute a hardly calculable percentage.

Many eyewitnesses including police and civil defence personnel gave evidence stating that there was **no panic** before the accident.

On the day after the tragedy, the government ordered Bethnal Green Borough Council to immediately implement all the measures the Borough Engineer had suggested. The local council was reimbursed the cost of these works but were threatened with the Official Secrets Act and so were forced to take the blame, indeed at a court case a few months later they were not even allowed to defend themselves in court! The case was held behind closed doors but the judge insisted that the summing up and conclusions be made public. Bethnal Green Borough Council over the years paid out compensation totalling £69,613.14s.4d, the equivalent in today's value of over £1.5 million, again giving the impression that they were at fault, however, the Government was quietly over time reimbursing the council. What a terrible burden this must have been for the councillors and particularly for the Borough Engineer who had tried so hard to get permission to prevent such a tragedy happening. Ironically, now whenever you descend the steps into an underground station you will see that there are adequate hand rails, lights and steps that are kept in good repair, all as a result of that terrible night.

It is presumed that the Home Secretary, Herbert Morrison, was lucky enough to have a cold the day he was due to deliver his final statement on the incident to Parliament thus preventing any awkward questions being raised. In his absence, someone else read out his words. One wonders what answers he would have given to any questions raised if he had been present in the House of Commons that day – one of the great 'what ifs' of World War Two.

Stairway to Heaven Memorial 2014

Lethal entrance to the Tube station c.1942

Workmen fitting replacement 'rails'. The actual site of the disaster – imagine over 173 bodies of people piled here, dead or struggling to avoid suffocation.

But out of evil often comes good. As a direct consequence of this disaster, tube stations across the Metropolis were given either improved or new handrails and step-edge markings.

19

The Last Three Years of World War Two

Towards the end of 1943, Ted came home on leave and, as planned, Vera came to London to stay the weekend with Ted's Dad and step-mother. Margaret was living at home but, unbeknown to her parents, she had started flat-hunting; however with huge swathes of East London having been flattened by bombs, accommodation was at a premium. Vera and Margaret spent some time together as they usually did, catching up on each other's news and, although Margaret was really excited, she did not give any hint of her brother's plans for the coming Sunday to Vera.

The next morning, Ted asked Vera to go for their normal walk but this day seemed different to Vera so she asked where they were going. "Just wait and see," grinned Ted. "It's a surprise."

Suddenly they turned the corner and Ted steered Vera towards a little Jewish family jewellers. The shop sold new and old jewellery including many pawned items. Ted stood her in front of the shop window and told her to choose a ring. Vera was speechless at first and just looked up at Ted's face.

He smiled and said, "Well, after the war we are going to get married so we should at least get engaged for now."

Vera looked at all the jewellery displayed in the shop window her eyes alighting on one particular ring which she knew at once was the ring she wanted. They went inside and Vera tried on the ring. It was a little small but the jeweller obligingly stretched it while they waited. Vera and Ted smiled all the way home and were met at the door by an excited Margaret. "Well?" she said, smiling at them.

Without a word, Vera smiled back and held out her left hand to show Margaret her engagement ring.

"Congratulations to you both, I am so pleased for you and guess what?"

"What?" the engaged pair asked together. "I have just got back from seeing a flat for Bert and I."

Ted and Vera returned the congratulation.

Then Margaret smiled and said, "So who is going to tell Lizzie first?"

Margaret giggled as she asked this final question – she knew that Lizzie liked to know everything first and would be very displeased to know she had been kept in the dark by both of her step-children.

The war continued unabated although by the end of 1943 Londoners were noticing that the air raids were becoming less frequent. At the start of 1944, Germany again stepped up the bombing of London. This period became known as 'The Little Blitz'. Then on 13 June 1944, the German war machine deployed a new deadly menace.

Heard for the first time was the throbbing drone of a pulse-jet in the sky – then suddenly, the noise would cease and within moments a huge single explosion would rent the air as the unmanned (*Vergeltungswaffe* – Revenge Weapon) V1 rocket, having run out of fuel, or having reached its pre-set target area, dived to earth.

Near the railway arch in Grove Road there is a blue plaque at the landing site of the first V1 which killed 6 people and injured a further 30 as well as leaving almost 200 people homeless. It was one of ten rockets launched from across the channel and it was the only one to hit its original target. Within days, many more of these rockets, nicknamed 'Doodlebugs' fell on London.

In Bethnal Green, as in other parts of East London and further afield, people were again forced to flee from the new threat to life, this time wrought by the V1s This new weapon was a flying bomb that resembled an aeroplane but without a pilot! The arrival of this new missile in the German arsenal was to heighten fear in the British public as no one could be sure when the engine would cut out nor where its final destination would be. The only certainty was that, once the V1 fell silent, an explosion would quickly follow from the one ton bomb together with immense destruction. A natural instinct when you heard the drone of the rocket was to pray that it would pass you by and fall harmlessly onto a bombsite and for those that found themselves on the flight paths the only safe choice was a return to underground shelters, spending as much time as possible in there.

With the arrival of the V1, it became apparent that a new strategy was required to combat these, The British Government fed false target information to the Germans and took the decision to move anti-aircraft guns out of London and from the rest of the country into the countryside, south of London. Kent at this period became known as 'bomb alley' as large quantities of the V1 rockets were brought down in mainly open countryside. Our fastest fighters including the brand new Meteor jets were also deployed to shoot down or 'tip' the rocket planes so that their gyro mechanism caused the flying bomb to dive to destruction. This does not mean there were no civilian casualties resultant from this new strategy though. Vera, living and working on the land in Kent witnessed many incidents of rockets being deflected or brought down near Tonbridge.

On 6 June 1944, the Allies landed on the Normandy beaches in northern France; this foothold   eventually enabled the destruction of the V1 launch site in the Pas de Calais region (there were others and these too were gradually destroyed as the Allies moved east). Londoners were ecstatic when news of this became known but the delight within a few months turned to renewed fear when in September ominous explosions began to pound the earth on the perimeter of London.

A new even deadlier rocket, the V2, was the cause. It was larger and more powerful than its predecessor with a far greater range travelling at supersonic speeds, and indeed was the first missile to momentarily leave the earth's atmosphere. The V2 was silent until it exploded, the first awareness of its impact being the brilliant flash of light and deafening explosion. Moments later came the eerie whoosh of its descent as the sound waves caught up.

Between September 1944 and March 1945 approximately 500 V2 rockets fell on London, though many of these being were targeted at central London, Bethnal Green also took further punishment. The government, fearing public reaction to the arrival of the V2 rockets initially broadcast the news that the unexplained noises were faulty gas pipes – however, the public were not fooled and with typical Cockney humour would soon, upon hearing an explosion, look up and say, "There goes another flying gas pipe!"

Two months after the first 'rocket' attack, Hitler announced details of the rocket's capabilities and the British Government was then forced into admitting that the country had been under rocket attack for two months. The rockets were not launched from static sites but as the Allied armies pushed the Germans back, the mobile rocket launchers became useless as the designers were incapable of lengthening the delivery target range.

There remains some global debt to the V2 rocket research, for the missiles were the forerunners of modern day rockets developed by the USA and USSR after the war ended, assisted by captured German scientists. There was one final weapon to be aimed at the Allies, and that was the V3, but this weapon had a faulty design. The V3 was essentially a gigantic gun with rocket assisted propulsion, which led to instability when fired, often causing the rocket-shell to land harmlessly far short of its target, if it left the 'gun' at all.

The start of World War Two was heralded by a very hot summer but the last winter of the war was the coldest ever recorded. A shortage of fuel meant, for many, sacrificing many personal items to the fire to keep warm. Fresh food shortages became acute as vegetables were frozen solid in the ground. One delight for school children was the discovery that the ink in the inkwells had frozen! With the war now virtually over, life started to return to some semblance of pre-war normality. Gradually blackout regulations were withdrawn, barrage balloons were taken down, underground tube stations reverted to train stations from shelters and, most welcoming of all, street lights came on and street signs were restored.

On 1 May 1945, the news was announced that Hitler was dead. A woman in East London listened to the radio announcement in disbelief, then ran to her neighbours to tell her the momentous news, they hugged each other in sheer delight and in typical East London style then shared a bottle of Guinness that the neighbour had been saving for a special occasion. Barbara Nichol's was getting ready to go to Girl Guides that evening when her mother called up the stairs to her, "That bloody Hitler's dead, he took poison!"

In fact he shot himself. It seems he did not like the way his pet dog had reacted to a poison capsule. The top of his shattered skull is said to have been kept on Stalin's desk for many years.

On 8 May 1945, the cessation of hostilities with Germany was formally announced following Germany's surrender.

Barbara's father, like many others, put on all the lights in the house to celebrate; he also managed to find a huge Union Jack flag that he proudly hung across the front of the house. The daily newspaper headlines announced a two-day public holiday and people went wild with joy and happiness. The war was finally over... they danced in the streets, hugging loved ones as well as strangers in the exuberance of the moment. Ships on the Thames fired rockets into the sky in celebration, boats sounded their horns and everywhere a great sense of elation enveloped a war-weary nation.

Many Londoners, including those living in Bethnal Green, made their way to the centre of London ('Up West' as they termed it) to join in the euphoria that had suddenly taken hold of every citizen in the country. The streets were tightly packed with huge crowds of people linking arms, singing, laughing and cheering. Locals joined with allied troops stationed in London to celebrate as different nationalities became one writhing mass of humanity, suddenly let loose from the scourge of war. Strangers could be seen dancing in the streets, shaking hands and hugging

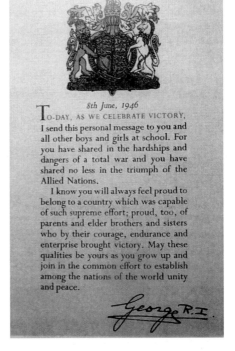

8th June, 1946
TO-DAY, AS WE CELEBRATE VICTORY, I send this personal message to you and all other boys and girls at school. For you have shared in the hardships and dangers of a total war and you have shared no less in the triumph of the Allied Nations.

I know you will always feel proud to belong to a country which was capable of such supreme effort; proud, too, of parents and elder brothers and sisters who by their courage, endurance and enterprise brought victory. May these qualities be yours as you grow up and join in the common effort to establish among the nations of the world unity and peace.

George R.I.

each other in the sheer joy of it all. They sang as one voice that night all the war songs that has sustained them through six long years. As a two day national holiday had been declared, numerous street parties were organised with flags and bunting draped from house to house. Meanwhile Margaret held her own special celebration on the day war ended with the birth of her first child, Peter.

Barbara Nichol and her sister Jean were taken from Bethnal Green to Piccadilly Circus by their aunt to watch and join in the celebrations. Barbara clearly remembers seeing the red-headed showgirl Zoe Gail on a balcony in Piccadilly Circus with the surrounding searchlights trained on her as she sang the pop song of the time: *I am going to get lit up when the lights go up in London.*

An acquaintance, as a child in 1945, recalled the relief felt by many that they no longer needed to live with the constant fear of sirens sounding out warnings of air raids. For the children – many of whom had only ever known rationing – school parties were organised and each child was given a special illuminated celebratory letter from the King.

During the war, Bethnal Green suffered huge damage from German air attacks. An estimated 80 tons (72,575kg) of bombs including parachute mines, oil bombs, flying bombs, long-range rockets and incendiaries were dropped on the area. A total of 555 people had been killed and 400 were seriously injured. One of the fatalities had been a good friend of Mrs Nichol (who had killed when the first V1 fell at Grove Road) she had been in the shop next to the bridge at the time. Approximately 21,000 houses were hit and of those 2,233 were destroyed with a further 893 becoming uninhabitable during war-time as a result of bombing raids.

20

Post-War Living

The war had ended but all around the East End of London the horrific devastation was clear to see with huge areas bombed to obliteration. Food was still rationed, indeed some items would continue to be rationed until 1954, but the population had become used to making do with whatever meagre portions of food were available, and inevitably many people were malnourished and sleep deprived after nearly six years of war.

In 1945, after the cessation of war, Britain was heavily in debt and it would be December 2006 before the final debt was cleared. By the end of the war, the cost of the conflict to the country was twice that of World War One, and in addition, many of Britain's overseas assets had been sold to finance the war. Other possessions had become liabilities rather assets, so the Empire moved towards becoming a Commonwealth of independent nations. At home the country also had to pay for the cost of rebuilding the nation especially in areas such as Bethnal Green that had sustained such a great deal of bomb damage.

It was not just homes that were lacking – all homes needed furnishing. In 1942, the government realised that the shortage of material to produce furniture (coupled with a shortage of second-hand furniture due to bombing) meant they needed to form a plan of action now - not only for those households needing replacement furniture but also for newly married couples. Thus the Utility Furniture Scheme was born. New furniture was rationed and was restricted to newly-weds and people who had been bombed out under the *Domestic Furniture (Control of Manufacture and Supply (No 2) Order, 1942)*, operative from 1 November 1942. In 1943, 'The Utility Furniture Catalogue' was produced with a small but reasonable range of plain design furniture (no embellishments were allowed in order to keep the quantity of materials required to a minimum). To obtain any furniture, you would need to apply for a 'Utility Furniture Buying' permit – which worked in a similar way to food and clothing coupons. My own parents bought utility furniture for their bedroom when they married, some of which my mum still has. The scheme continued until 1952. During the war, Utility clothing had also been introduced to ensure people were adequately clothed due to there being both material and labour shortages as production for the consumer had given way to the war effort. The Utility Clothing also carried the same logo as the furniture – C C (known as the two cheeses).

In 1945, Barbara reached school leaving age (14) and became apprenticed to a court dressmaker where she earned 15 shillings (75p) per week. When she started work, unlike today, she did not have any opportunity to buy new clothes to start her adult life. Instead, she continued to wear her school blazer and knee high socks as did many school leavers, at that time. Barbara's dressmaking skills were to be put to good use in 1949 when she stepped in to help her sister have a white wedding.

Many children had suffered almost constant disruption to their education during the war. Often as the siren sounded, teachers would rush the children to some form of shelter and in the haste to reach safety, books would be abandoned in the classroom. Frequently the price children paid in this period was to leave school without any qualifications.

Just after the war ended, Aunt Lydie became concerned for her husband Ted's health. He had begun to slur his speech and found the ability to control movement difficult. At first it was thought that the constant broken nights of sleep with fire-watching duty, the need for vigilance at all times, frequent air raids and trying to carry on working during the day had all taken their toll. Gradually his health declined further and although the diagnosis of his illness at that time was given a different name, he was in fact suffering from Motor Neurone Disease. He became bed-ridden as his legs and arms lost their use and his speech became incoherent leaving him angrily frustrated as he struggled to make himself understood. Aunt Lydie nursed her husband devotedly.

Young Ted would call on his aunt, uncle and cousin whenever he could and helped his aunt take uncle Ted to hospital for appointments, which must have been extremely difficult given the patients inability to walk. Aunt Lydie did manage to acquire a wheelchair for her husband and this gave them all a little more freedom.

Uncle Ted died at the beginning of 1946, leaving his family heartbroken. To give an insight into the harshness of people's lives during this time, I mention here Lydie's experience when she sought financial aid. Newly widowed and with a child to care for, she applied for financial assistance; however, when the 'Assistance' people called on her they noticed the wheelchair in the corner of the room. She was asked if she owned the wheelchair and confirming she did was then advised to sell it and use the cash from the sale before reapplying for 'assistance'.

Many people suffered illness post-war as a direct result of the war's stresses. I will use my father (Ted Overy) as an example of the many who suffered in this way. He had been discharged from the Army in 1946 with a fine reference both to his personality and his abilities, he was however a very, very tired man leaving him prone to infection that an otherwise healthy young man could have shrugged off. Soon after being demobbed, he cut himself shaving – a harmless enough and regular occurrence then, given the type of razor blades in use at that time. He treated the cut with antiseptic and thought nothing more of this incident, but gradually his health deteriorated until he was admitted to the local Bancroft Hospital in Stepney with severe septicaemia. For weeks he was an in-patient and his life hung in the balance but the skill of the doctors and nursing staff saved his life, together with the wonder drug penicillin. Without this new discovery he would, like many others, have died.

Despite the debt the nation owed Winston Churchill as wartime leader, his party was heavily defeated in 1945 in the first election since the war had begun. Though early planning had been carried out in the Churchill era the Labour Party brought in a world standard set of innovations and reforms on the principle that the population should be provided for 'from the cradle to the grave'. There were costs involved, of course.

On 5 July 1946, the National Health Act was introduced giving the population 'free' medical care for the first time. The report by the Inter-Departmental Committee on Social Insurance and Allied Services, known as the Beveridge Report, paved the way for the National Health Act. During the committee's deliberations, 'five giant evils' in society were identified – squalor, ignorance, want, idleness and disease. The remedies recommended were widespread reform of the social welfare system. The government's public relations department at the time gave a promise to the country to implement reforms as a reward for the sacrifices made by the citizens during the war and the news was greeted with great enthusiasm by the majority of the populace. There were other Acts of Parliament brought into being following on from the recommendations of the Beveridge Report, including the

Family Allowance Act 1945; National Insurance (Industrial Injuries) Act 1946; and the National Insurance Act 1946.

Thousands of those who had survived were now homeless, in fact, of all the depredations suffered by local people, homelessness was the greatest hardship. Much of the housing had been substandard but at least it had been home. Now the Town Hall faced an unprecedented challenge to find accommodation for the homeless but their efforts on behalf of the local population were not appreciated as many of the indigenous population felt betrayed by the lack of sensitivity shown to them. My own family testified to the general consensus of being let down, ignored and treated as just another statistic rather than as human beings. With hindsight, the rebuilding of such a heavily bombed area as Bethnal Green, given the bankrupt state of the country at the end of the war, was a mammoth task and enormous resources were needed in order to achieve the goal. Even so, Bethnal Greeners and other East Enders undoubtedly paid a very high price in every aspect of this project.

To begin with, people were encouraged to move in with family or friends but the council also looked to a temporary solution to this mass accommodation crisis in the form of 'pre-fabricated' housing. The 'Prefab' was a single storey dwelling hut, consisting of a kitchen, one or two bedrooms, a living room and a bathroom – this last room was quite novel to many families who were used to a weekly ablution in a tin bath in front of the fire not to mention an outside toilet in the backyard. The 'Prefab' was wired for electricity and there were hot water facilities, unheard of at this time in the area.

Soon these dwellings were being mass produced, delivered and erected on bomb sites all around the East End. The prefab was intended to be a temporary solution to the acute post-war housing shortage but quite a number of these were in use for up to thirty years, and even today this brilliant design can still be found in small mature, much sought after, 'bungalow' estates half a century after being built. Large numbers of families were delighted with their new, albeit 'temporary' homes, much to the surprise of local officials but these officials had not lived in damp, cramped, amenity lacking accommodation, and many of them did not even live in the area so could not visualise the contrast these basic homes offered.

Many families suffered the austerity of post-war Britain with rationing still being part of everyday life but not all families struggled. Pam was an only child who was still living in a 'Prefab' in Water Road, Bethnal Green. Pam and her parents lived a reasonably comfortable life at this time, they even had a car. Their old home had suffered bomb damage and they were moved into the prefab in 1945. The prefabs may have been small but large family parties could still be accommodated in them.

Following the inception of the Town & Country Planning Act 1947, giving compulsory purchasing powers to local authorities and the LCC. Decisions were then taken by the town planners whether to demolish all, or just badly damaged, properties in an area. It was decided that in some cases, even properties that could be repaired would be demolished in the planners' desire for a new East End. Many fine properties were lost to the wholesale destruction of large parts of Bethnal Green and other areas of East London, and with the demolition of these properties, unwittingly the death of whole communities was sanctioned too. Many people from Bethnal Green as in other parts of East London were given priority housing status if they chose to move out of the borough to places such as the new purpose-built post-war estates outside of London and although they loved their new homes with proper amenities, they were unhappy to leave Bethnal Green and sorely missed their old neighbours. Yes, there had been many sub-standard properties, without basic facilities that we would today take for granted such as hot water but instead of rebuilding proper city homes the people were offered newly-built high rise 'flats' or as the architects and planners named them – 'Streets in the Sky'.

Hitler, it was said, had rid the East End of bugs, but it would seem to some that the town hall planners were intent upon wreaking their own destruction in their quest for what they deemed 'good-quality' housing. This remit even included some of the late nineteenth century purpose built apartment blocks such as Merceron House on the junction of Victoria Park Square and Globe Road with its beautiful yellow and red brick façade, built by the East End Dwellings Company in 1901 for poorer residents. In 1949 the building was razed to the ground rather than being modernized, and was then rebuilt. Fortunately, not all of the East End was 'blitzed' by the town hall planners and although far too many buildings were torn down, the few surviving are a reminder of the old pre-war Bethnal Green in the East End.

For many residents, the task of rebuilding post-war Bethnal Green was to bring immense changes not only to the landscape of the area but to their way of life. Prior to this, families had always lived close to one another. The mother of the family often played a key role in assisting the younger generation in many aspects of life. A high proportion of families still lived in rented accommodation with houses frequently accommodating several generations of one family (as had been the case with my own family, the Nortons, in Approach Road). Many women maintained a friendly relationship with the local rent collector as well as keeping an ear to the local grapevine in order to perhaps be given first refusal of any accommodation becoming available in the vicinity for her married or soon to be married children.

With accommodation being at a premium, even before the ravages of the *Blitz*, it was increasingly difficult for couples to source a home of their own so when couples married they tended to start married life mainly with the wife's family in a couple of rooms and would share the communal facilities such as the kitchen. I say mainly but if you were one of several daughters then a lack of space in your parents' home would mean either starting married life with your husband's parents or postponing your wedding until alternative accommodation could be found. Some rented accommodation would be tenanted by the same family over several generations – as the oldest tenant died the next of kin, also being resident in the home, would automatically seek to have their name as the principal tenant on the rent book going forwards. This close proximity living of families allowed the members of the family to interact with and help each other in many ways, such as child care and care of the elderly members of the family.

In planning this new town from the ashes of the old, four themes were considered: traffic congestion, the cheek-by-jowl existence of business and residential properties, the lack of open spaces and shortage of housing. The traffic congestion worsened following the 'improvements'. Businesses were encouraged to move out of the area into suburban districts leaving their workers, who had traditionally taken a pedestrian route to work, without adequate means of travel to their employers' new premises.

Although not all employees were faced with an impossible journey as many small businesses such as book binding and furniture making continued to thrive, it was a common sight in the first half of the 20th Century to see carts trundling along the streets piled high with table and chair legs, table tops, shelves, doors and cabinets – all being transported to subcontractors for assembly.

Planners 'solved' the lack of open spaces by building tower blocks of various heights and surrounding these with small patches of green rather than rebuild the old system of streets which had given the area such character and encouraged strong family communities.

The new Bethnal Green, as did other parts of the East End, was beginning to look like a series of boxes of diverse sizes, all built on a very tight budget that did not allow for good quality local amenities such as shops and schools. Many locals mourned the passing of their community and felt no loyalty to these soulless boxes in the sky. Tower blocks can be and often are beautifully constructed with good quality materials and attention to the needs of those who will either live or work there. However, many of the early post-war East End tower blocks were very badly constructed with cheap materials and paper thin walls, giving many new residents in this type of accommodation a feeling of isolation once you shut your front door. Gone was the elderly resident who would be regularly visited by a neighbour; people began to lead a more introverted lifestyle and in so doing lost a valuable quality of life that had been an intrinsic part of the East End. As mentioned earlier, many families decided to move out and rebuild their lives in suburbia; the chance to leave cramped, damp accommodation lacking basic amenities such as hot running water and their own toilet was a dream many decided to, if they could, turn into reality unless you were from the 'poor' class in society. The downside that such a move meant was to sacrifice some of the old ways of living in Bethnal Green and other parts of East London that they had known – especially the nearby close family and friend ties they had grown up with.

My parents to be, Ted and Vera married in June 1946. They honeymooned for a week in the 'family' favourite seaside resort – Ramsgate. On the second day they met up with Phoebe and Charles Kerridge who were also on holiday with their little son Victor (Vicky) who had been born in 1943. My dad, throughout his life, had a great love of children, and they adored him.

Vicky spent the morning happily playing with Ted (my dad) and as they sat down to lunch young Vicky turned to my mum and asked, "Can I play with your boy again this afternoon?"

The newly-weds were forced to live apart for the first nine months of their marriage due to the chronic post-war housing shortage; however, Ted's Uncle Walter heard on the 'grapevine' of a basement flat for rent within a three-storey townhouse in Chobham Road Stratford E15. The house was owned by a middle-aged spinster who lived on the upper floors and was, by definition of her behaviour, a little eccentric. The accommodation was small but, with a little decoration, would be cosy for the time being so Ted enthusiastically got to work on the redecoration only to find the landlady keen to assist – by scraping off the old wallpaper using a knife and fork...

My parents had only expected to rent this flat for a short while but it was 10 years before they were able to find a more suitable home and, of course, their experience was one that many couples had to endure immediately post-war. During their tenancy, the owner became increasingly mentally unstable until it was no longer viable for her to care for herself. She was admitted to Goodmayes Mental Hospital where she lived for a number of years. During her hospitalisation, she wrote to Ted and asked him to visit her which he did; however, at the end of the visit she offered to show him a quick way out.

"Don't worry," she said. "I always go out through the gap in the wire fence to buy my cigarettes."

Ted often wondered after that if the authorities ever became aware of the in-patient short-cut from the secure hospital unit!! He decided against further visits in case he was caught leaving by this unorthodox route.

I had been born in Stratford in September 1950. A few months earlier in April of that year Margaret had given birth to a second child, my cousin Sheila. Both my cousin and I were born at home, which was still a quite normal occurrence with midwives travelling about on their bikes – a regular sight. Often the mother-to-be's mother or another close relative that lived nearby would help the new mother for a few days after the birth.

Sheila made a fairly dramatic entrance into this world; her mother was helped that day by her own sister-in-law Lena who quickly named the new arrival Sheila as she was not expected to survive. My birth apparently was a long and difficult labour during which time neighbours came to offer 'support' to my dad while he awaited the baby's arrival.

The neighbour, listening at the bedroom door, gave a running commentary as the actual birth drew near and unfortunately misheard the midwife's comment – "A girl, bald head." Instead, the neighbour informed Ted: "A girl, born dead."

For a few seconds my father must have been distraught beyond measure, but only for a few moments before he heard the healthy cry of a new-born child! I had arrived.

As a child in the 1950s, my parents and I regularly visited Bethnal Green and other parts of East London where family members still lived. I remember walking past areas left almost as they were when the bombs fell, giving the appearance of a time capsule. I never thought then of the people that had lived and possibly died there during the war nor of the awful sights they must have witnessed during that terrible period. Harry Hunt, who had joined the Royal Air Force as a seventeen year old had then immediately been posted to the Far East, not returning to these shores until he was twenty-two years old. He recalled how he had been extremely shocked to see the devastation that had been wrought in his home town.

Many other areas were flattened and remained so for quite a while – these areas were a favourite of the children who at that time did not have much open space to play on.

"Let's go play on the bomb site!" was an idea called out in every war-damaged town and city, for the start of imaginative play and mischief.

Another favourite 'playground' haunt for local children was the by then derelict *Columbia Road Market* – where children loved to play in the large empty space until it was demolished in 1952.

Meanwhile some family members were in time rehoused in the new post-war blocks of flats. I recall my cousin Gloria, who with her parents were rehoused from Morris House to James Hammett House on the newly built Dorset Estate. *The Hackney Gazette* reported in an article, *The laying of the foundation stone of the Dorset Estate by the Mayor*, in its edition 23 March 1953, that the accommodation within each block would be very modern and served with the unheard of luxury then for working-class people – central heating, provided by hot-water coils embedded in the ceilings of the halls and living rooms and was believed to be the first time such a form of heating has been built into a housing scheme. The estate was named in memory of the six 'Tolpuddle Martyrs' who had pioneered the Trade Union movement. *The Hackney Gazette* was also there to record the opening of this Estate in its paper in March 1958.

Gloria said how she had loved to visit me at our new home in south-east London after we moved there in 1956 because I had a garden! I never realised how lucky I was to have a garden, instead I felt such joy when visiting her as we ran out to play on the green or in nearby Victoria Park. When we visited each other with our parents, we nearly always used to 'persuade' our mum and dad to let us have an overnight stay – it was such fun to do.

Often we, that is mum, dad and I, could be found visiting relatives in Bethnal Green. We would take the train to London Bridge and then a bus across London. I used to love these rides and always asked if we could go upstairs as I enjoyed seeing the ever changing scenery as we travelled across London.

As many of the family lived near each other it was not uncommon to call in and see several families while we were in an area. This way we would frequently have spontaneous get-togethers. I was about 8 years old when we visited Phoebe and Charles Deeks one Sunday morning and found Phoebe, Charles and their son Vicky had also arrived. Then Vic, Joyce and Gloria unexpectedly called in too. It was near to Guy Fawkes Night so Old Aunt Phoebe (as she was known) gave Vicky some money and told him to take Gloria and me to the local shop to buy us each a packet of sparklers.

Gloria and I happily trotted alongside our older and taller cousin to the shop but on the way back Vicky, who was always full of fun, suddenly held the packets high above his head and laughingly invited us to try to take a packet from him. We tried hard to jump high and get our prize with Vicky just laughing loudly at our attempts as he raised the prizes higher.

He teased us all the way back to his Gran's then, still smiling; let us have a packet each. Great fun, we thought, and loved him for it. Children during that era had a much more simplistic outlook on life and would enjoy simple pranks be they the giver or receiver.

December 1952 and the particularly cold winter saw the 'Great Smog' as it became known. The cold weather, combined with an anticyclone plus windless conditions, and the almost universal use of fossil fuels, allowed air-borne pollutants to gather and swirl around in the atmosphere thickening it into a man-made fog (smog). These 'peasoupers', as they became known, had occurred in earlier years but this time the dense yellow smog lasted from 5-9 December after which the smog dispersed with a change in the weather.

The pollutants were mainly from the high domestic consumption of coal in the weeks preceding the arrival of the Great Smog. Post-war domestic coal was a low grade sulphurous variety, for economic reasons the higher grade coal mined in the UK was exported. The sulphur from the coal burning coupled with the diesel fuelled buses, was to have a serious effect on people's respiratory systems with many resultant fatalities. Visibility was reduced to just a few yards making any journey hazardous, and even the emergency services struggled to provide a proper service.

Bus conductors walked in front of their buses, each carrying a lighted torch to give a little visibility to the driver. After darkness, travelling by foot or transport became even more hazardous as street lights were not designed at that time to penetrate fog/smog. Some people purchased 'smog masks' from the local chemist to try to alleviate the effect on their breathing.

The long term benefits from this peril were the implementation of the Clean Air Act in 1956 which enforced a reduction of air pollution and an offer of financial incentives to householders to switch to either coke (a cleaner alternative) or to install gas fires. This man-made disaster was to have another long reaching effect as it gave birth to the Environment movement who began to raise concerns about various pollutants and other environmentally unfriendly issues.

Ted remembered trying to walk along the street in the smog it was a far from pleasant experience and not always easy to find your destination even in familiar surroundings. One could lose bearings on the turning of a corner. Barbara Nichol vividly recalls being very worried when her dad failed to arrive home one evening during the Great Smog. Barbara's mother had died in May 1952 leaving Barbara to take over running the household and caring for her dad but her sister and her husband lived in the first floor flat above. Finally came a knock on the door. When Barbara opened the door, she was shocked to see her dad collapse into the hallway. He was unable to get his breath and had struggled to make his way home. He had weak lungs through gas inhalation during World War One and the effects of the smog induced Bronchitis would eventually lead to Emphysema and an early death in 1961.

Another evening Barbara opened the door to find a soaking wet and bedraggled sister Jean on the doorstep – she had fallen into the boating lake in Victoria Park after losing her way. The smog insidiously crept into every nook and cranny, it was impossible to stop it permeating the house. On waking sleepers could find their nostrils clogged with the intake of particles in the air. Even cinemas were forced to close if the smog gained entry.

Interestingly, an employer of Barbara was the renowned Dr Bronowski whose scientific detective work helped to lead the way in discovering the causes of smog. Part of Barbara's job was to collect the special filters on chimneys the doctor had developed to attempt to ascertain what manner of particles were polluting the atmosphere from various coal products burned in the fireplaces of the building.

Slowly as the new decade of the 50s progressed, the population began to pick up the threads of normal everyday life. Many firms in the post-war years such as Charrington's the Brewery, which had lost a large proportion of its public houses due to bomb damage, were beginning to recover. Charrington's even purchased three large independent brewing firms to increase their business. I found a description of street life as viewed from the top of a bus travelling down Bethnal Green Road in the 1950s:

> *You do not have to live in Bethnal Green, you only have to take a bus down the main street, to notice that this is a place of many industries. You pass tailors' workshops, furniture makers and Kearly & Tonge's food warehouse, all near to Allen & Hanbury's big factory.*

Bethnal Green could be presented in the early 1950s as a good place to live. The streets might be crowded with stalls but they were bearable because practically no one in Bethnal Green owned a motorcar! Strong local loyalties and a respectable working class that still took pride in its doorstep scrubbing in areas such as Mace Street and Gibraltar Walk gave stability to the area which was described in 1951 as orderly and safe. Most people had been born in the borough, like their parents and probably grandparents, and lived near their relatives. The wife's mother, as mentioned earlier, was often the nucleus of family life.

Small workshops in the many buildings left empty by bombing and slum clearance offered a variety of jobs for men and part-time work for women. My uncle, Vic Deeks, had a small woodcarving workshop in Swanfield Street. Local people still valued and were proud of many of the local trades. Pam, who had left school in 1956, became apprenticed to a bookbinder in Bishops Way, Bethnal Green. Aunt Lydie was working for Kearly & Tonge in the 1950s from where she ordered a beautiful crinoline doll birthday cake for Gloria's 8th birthday. Other local employers in the area were – Allen & Hanbury Ltd, a well-known chemical manufacturer and surgical instrument maker with premises in Three Colts Lane; The Emerald Furniture Co. Ltd., formed by demobbed men in

1949, producing high-quality upholstery; and Stamford Metallics Ltd., who manufactured clockwork motors for a wide range of children's toys. These few examples show that local employment was still possible and that there was a wide diversity of trades.

The unemployment and grinding labour of earlier periods were over. During the inter-war years a gradual reduction in working hours, hastened by the years of depression and unemployment, had become the norm and by 1948 many occupations allowed employees a six or even a five-day working week which in itself wrought changes to family life. Pre-war, no man was seen pushing a pram on a Saturday or walking along with his wife to the shops but post-war this became acceptable. People who had been educated during the inter-war years began to value the chance they had been given of a regular education. Maybe not everyone was grateful but people's attitudes to the opportunities an education could offer did change and many fathers wanted their sons (sadly, it was still a little early for daughters to be given equal status) to acquire a 'good' education and for it to lead to a well-paid job.

Prior to World War Two, sons had often followed their fathers into the same form of work, even if sometimes it was for a different employer, though the father usually recommended his son to his employer. Post-war, this trend slowly began to decline with many sons seeking employment in offices and banks or working for the town council. This shift in work opportunities would have been unheard of before the Second World War. Several members of my family subsequently chose a white-collar career route post-war.

People were wanting a better life for their children in other ways too, with the limiting of family numbers to a more manageable size in the post-Victorian era. Parents had time to consider other aspects of family life and the roles of parents began to change slowly as they began to take joint decisions regarding the purchase of, say, luxury items – such as a television or a radiogram. Barbara Nicol's parents saved hard to buy a radiogram; they wanted their daughters' to enjoy life as much as possible and would encourage them to bring their friends home for evenings to listen to the radiogram.

Birth and death rates had fallen, leaving fewer widows and orphans, and the advent of television was beginning to weaken the draw of the public house as the key place for entertainment. Interaction between husband and wife also started to change as women were now encouraged to go out to work thus increasing the income of the family. Before the war women were expected to cease working once they married as the husband was deemed the provider, although women often undertook low-paid homework or took in washing to bring in a few extra 'coppers' (old pence). The war needs had required many many women to fill the vacancies left by men drafted into the services and having taken on the men's jobs in factories, offices and on farms. Women suddenly found they were no longer tied to the home but encouraged to go out and earn a living in spite of being married. Women felt more emancipated than ever.

When their husbands returned home after the war, they were able to resume their old jobs but women began to seek part-time work and as there was a shortage of man-power post-war female employment was not discouraged. My mum, Vera, had after her marriage various employments in East London until I was born. One employment of Vera's was piece work at a brush factory. The hours were long and the pay very low so many of these workers would at the end of the week take home components to assemble brushes and earn a few extra shillings (5p equals 1 shilling) overtime, but they often took home a few extra that had already been assembled (well, the pay was a pittance) so were in effect paid twice.

Young women were also advantaged in that shortly after the end of the war the need for a large Army called for National Service. Every young man in the country, if fit for duty, and most were, served two compulsory years in the Armed Forces. This carried on until 1959. The perceived threat came from Stalin's USSR. The need for National Service eased with armed forces' pay rises bringing the development of an all-regular force. Later Germany began a rearmament programme as part of NATO so that numbers on the ground in Europe no long depended on the United Kingdom, France and the United States, alone.

A high proportion of the people living in Bethnal Green were from a working-class background who may not have been financially well-off but they were rich in many other ways. The bond of kinship was very strong and there was a great sense of pride amongst themselves in their community. The Jewish population had begun an exodus during World War Two. In 1948, it was estimated that 10 per cent (6,000) of the population was Jewish, mostly in the west and south of Bethnal Green, but this had decreased to just 8 per cent in 1955. Immigration from the Commonwealth had not by then had a great impact. In 1948 the *Empire Windrush* arrived and from it disembarked many Jamaicans who had been encouraged to travel to the UK to fill job vacancies. In 1954, it could be said that there was little colour prejudice because the non-European population was minute and there was little political or criminal violence. This was to change.

The growth of traffic led the council in 1959 to divert street trading to a new market off Roman Road. The number of dwellings in Bethnal Green declined from 15,854 in 1951 to 14,649 in 1961 by which time the population was contained in 5,729 buildings, 230 of them blocks of more than 10 dwellings.

Vera remembered starting out on married life in London and was very grateful to both family and friends helping her to adjust to an urban lifestyle. She and Phoebe Kerridge became good friends, Phoebe lived a short distance away in Chingford but often came back to her roots in Bethnal Green as many of her family and friends still lived there or in surrounding parts of East London. Wickhams – the East End Department Store – invited people to join their savings club and get their friends and family to pay into it; Phoebe ran the family's membership. Each would agree to pay in 1 shilling (5 pence in decimal money) each week, which may not sound much but wages were at that time no more than £5-7 per week. Phoebe collected the money and paid it over; weekly a draw would take place and the lucky person would be given the chance to spend £1 in the shop. They would in time have to pay off the £1 but it was a godsend to people needing to get this form of credit at that time.

In February 1952 King George VI died and his daughter

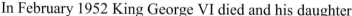

Above, Margaret at the foot of the left hand side of the photo, with her children Peter and Sheila, presumably watching an entertainer and myself (looking the wrong way) attending one of these street parties.

Elizabeth acceded the throne but it was not until 2 June 1953 that Queen Elizabeth's Coronation ceremony took place. At this time televisions became a little more affordable for the working classes and my own family purchased their first TV to watch the Coronation. The set had a black & white picture with a 9-inch (22.5cm) screen. The only broadcasting service at that time was the BBC (British Broadcasting Corporation). Ted and Vera invited Phoebe, Charles and their son Victor to their home to watch the Coronation. A common event across the country for those who had sets. We all excitedly gathered round this little box and watched history unfold before our eyes that day. The Coronation was a chance for people to celebrate and many street parties were organised, as shown on previous page. Many recently married couples were partying and watching that day.

Couples who had met during the war, or post-war, decided to marry just after the war ended – including Vicky Deeks to Joyce Devey. Joyce was touched by the kindness of her soon to be in-laws when her future mother-in-law asked to speak to her privately one day.

"Joyce, do you want to marry my son Vic?" asked Phoebe Deeks, "I just wondered as you have not set a wedding date yet."

Joyce thought for a moment then felt she would have to just be honest with Phoebe and explain why she had not as yet set a date. "Oh yes, I do want to marry your son but mum and gran can't afford the cost of the wedding so I am trying to save up as the bride's family traditionally pays for it."

Phoebe was probably ready for this and smiled, then said, "Oh, is that all? You just go and set the date and we will pay."

This generosity of older down to younger demonstrated the closeness of families from that part of London, they would always look after each other. No one had much but they would always share what they had with those they loved.

Joyce Deeks. Shortly after marriage.

They couple married in St Peter's Church Bethnal Green, on Boxing Day 1947, and had in time been blessed with a little girl, Gloria, born in April 1949.

Two more family weddings were celebrated when Eddy married Janet in 1950 and his brother Artie married Marcie in 1952. Each couple was eventually blessed with a daughter, Janice born to Eddy and Janet in 1957 and Rayna born to Artie and Marcie in 1961. As these two girls grew up they saw an East End very different from the one their fathers had known but Janice recalled her childhood as being a very happy one. I mention all of these joyful events here because it was a little unusual for so many weddings to take place in such a short space of time but many couples had been forced to put their wedding plans on hold until after the end of the war. The delay led to a sudden upturn in the numbers of couples setting a wedding date. It was very difficult to find special wedding anniversary cards in the shops for their 25th or 50th wedding anniversaries as manufacturers had not realised that weddings had peaked to such an extent post-war.

A later demographic consequence was a sudden pressure on school places in the 60s and 70s – that phenomena was countered by the arrival of the birth control pill and a consequent fall in the birth rate in the next few decades.

Another change that took place post-war was that it began to become fashionable for some couples to name their child with a name they preferred rather than automatically naming them for a family member. Most of my cousin's first names have not been family names.

Susie had met John in 1948. Both were good dancers and met at a dance hall, the *Hammersmith Palais*, one Saturday night. John, in all innocence, walked up to Susie and asked if he knew her as she looked like someone he knew. Susie thought he was just trying to chat her up so told him to go away. Fortunately he did not and they were married ten years later on 7 September 1958.

Many photos were taken that day but for me the best photo was of the four cousins, from the left here is Gloria, myself and Sheila with little Janice in front of me.

I was so excited as I had been chosen to be one of Susie's bridesmaids. Like earlier generations of the family I loved dressing up; we wore beautiful pale lemon dresses, a wreath of white flowers in our hair and little white gloves. I was always a skinny child but frequently hungry and while waiting for the bride to finish dressing, became unable to resist a salmon sandwich from a plate on the table. Hopefully no one noticed the slightly fishy smell of my gloves as I walked up the aisle behind my aunty. It was a wonderful day of which I have many special memories.

After Susie and John married, Aunt Lydie was informed by the local council that she would have to move into a one-bedroomed flat as she was now the sole occupant, so she moved for the final time in her life to Peabody Buildings in Bethnal Green.

Many changes were still taking place in the area as new immigrants from Pakistan moved in to live and work there in the 1950s.

With the war something of a distant memory, huge rebuilding programmes already finished or in progress helped bring new prosperity to our borough. The family, our extended family, so thoroughly stamped by its locality and the astonishing events of the century went from strength to strength. There being almost an imbalance of steady fortune. Then one day in the summer of 1960 I, as a young girl, heard the sound of crying. Tears were rare amongst us. But the family was about to be shaken to its core.

Vicky Kerridge, the son of Phoebe and Charles Kerridge, was a tall likable young man by then, popular with everyone especially with his younger cousins whenever we met. I remember him turning up and from no previous experience being better with a hula-hoop than I was - using my own hoop. We were all impressed by his keenness as a sportsman for he loved all water sports - fishing, diving, and swimming and, for us, the rather exotic sport of surfing. Phoebe, Charles and Vicky visited us the week before he and his parents went for a family holiday to Cornwall.

I was playing outside our sitting room window that day late in the holiday, a warm day so the window was open. It was then I heard the crying. I stopped playing and listened as I realised it was my dad! My dad, crying? My mum was there and she too clearly could not understand at first what he was trying to tell her but eventually she heard more clearly, so did I through the window, broken with sobs,

"Vicky has been drowned in Cornwall…it is all over the evening paper placards."

"Vicky?" I could hear my mother's gasp.

"Drowned!"

Mum was as shocked as Dad then and neither of them realised I was outside listening. Eventually I was told properly and can remember that awful feeling – already knowing but being told again, to this moment of writing.

The next day we all went to Vic and Joyce Deeks at their home. We did not have a telephone and naturally wanted to know if it really was true. Such a person to die like that, the possibility just could not be taken in. We learned, piece by piece, that Vicky had been out surfing and as he came ashore clutching his surfboard under one arm he waved to his mother sitting on the beach.

She naturally thought he was just waving a hello but he was really signalling that he was in trouble. Vicky was over 6 foot tall and was standing only knee deep in the water when he waved to his mother. Everything seemed natural then suddenly everyone realised he had fallen in some way, and had gone, out of sight!

His father's frantic attempt to get to Vicky and save him almost cost him his own life. Vicky was never seen again nor did the sea even return his body to shore. Death in the surf was not infrequent in Cornwall but his was the only body that year which was never recovered.

**Vicky Kerridge with
his adventure clothes
and that smile.**

Gloria, who was a first cousin of Vicky has written to me recalling the event. This kind of tragedy is never forgotten by members of a family. She wrote:

240

I also remember someone coming to our door and giving us the terrible news. My dad spent a lot of time down in Cornwall searching for him and also responding to calls from the police down there to identify people they had found in case one was Vicky. Sadly he was never found but as you know there is a grave in Cornwall and we have also had Phoebe's recorded on the stone there. (Phoebe died in 2013)

The parents could only put on a brave face, perhaps the only solace was being surrounded by the continuing vibrant life of our national and local recovery, with its continuous change. Though the family and extended family's love and support at this time was a great comfort to them and gave them the strength to go on.

By this time much was disappearing of the place in which all of us had grown and prospered. By 1962 a lot of the old street trades such as the knife grinder or the man selling fresh whelks and shrimps from his barrow were no longer in existence, but life evolves and often changes are good for an area. Such was already happening in Bethnal Green and was to continue until the present time.

21

Eating out – Bethnal Green style

E ast Londoners' culinary appetites have been
tempered over many decades by the migration of
many cultures into the area. A selection of the most famous
dishes, as you walk around the streets of Bethnal Green, can
still be consumed even if, in some cases, their original
businesses are no longer with us. It has been difficult to
choose a small and diverse selection for this chapter but,
keeping to the confines of the 100 years of history, I have
only mentioned a few of the well-known establishments that
would have been trading at least in part of this era.

Fish and chips: the very words conjure up a picture of hot
delicious battered fish with tasty fried potatoes eaten out of
the paper or people hurriedly leaving the premises for home
with their precious package, it certainly must be one of the
original takeaways. Potatoes had been introduced into
Britain by Sir Walter Raleigh but it is believed to be the
French who turned the humble potato into a chip and fried
it. In 1839 Charles Dickens mentions a 'fried fish
warehouse' in his novel *Oliver Twist*; East Londoners had
eaten fried fish sold by street sellers for decades. It is
rumoured that Angela Burdett-Coutts suggested that the two
items be put together giving us the truly British dish of fish
and chips. Whatever those who live in the north of England
may claim, East London was the setting for the first fish and
chip shop. Joseph Malin, an Ashkenazi Jewish immigrant
opened his shop in 1860 at 78 Cleveland Street near Bow;

shortly after he opened a further two shops in Old Ford Road, Bethnal Green and Globe Road, Mile End and so began the long marriage of fried fish and chips.

If we look back to Victorian Britain we see teeming streets but amongst the throng were many street traders such as pie-men walking about with their trays displaying their wares – pies filled with meat, fish or fruit. The meat pies were in that era usually filled with beef or mutton and the fruit pies would usually contain apples, damsons, cherries or currants; some of this fruit would have been grown locally in the Bethnal Green area. The fish pies were filled with eels which at that time arrived from Holland in Dutch barges that docked on the Thames at Lovat Lane, E3 near to Billingsgate Fish Market. The pie-men were a valuable source of inexpensive hot food for the poorer classes which made up a large percentage of the population of London. This really was the fast food of the Victorian age and very nourishing too.

Eels were a favourite dish of Londoners and were frequently accompanied by pea soup or parsley sauce - the latter was often served with chillies and vinegar and eventually this sauce became the famous liquor to accompany pies, mash and/or eels.

The pie-man was a great favourite with the public and so was the tradition of 'tossing the pie-man' whereby the customer would toss a coin and the pie-man would call heads or tails. If the pie-man's guess was correct then the customer owed the pie-man a penny but if the pie-man's guess was wrong then he would have to give his customer a free pie.

The demise of the street pie-man was brought about with the opening of the first eel, pie and mash shops with many a pie-man mourning the passing of their street trade. Kelly's business directory listed 33 eel, pie and mash shops in their 1874 edition.

Although individuals had opened eel, pie and mash shops, the first of the three main families in the eel, pie and mash trade were the Cookes who, according to family history, had opened their first shop in Sclater Street in 1862; over the years they have extended their business by opening several more shops around London.

The Manzes were the next family to found their own eel, pie and mash empire in London. The family had emigrated from Ravello in southern Italy and settled in Bermondsey, south London – taking up residence next door to the Cooke family. The eldest son of the Manzes - Michaele, had begun his working life as an ice cream merchant but felt he would like to diversify and noted the success that the eel, pie and mash shops were experiencing so, with advice from his neighbour Robert Cooke, he opened his first shop in 1902 in south London.

The third family of the eel, pie and mash empire are the Kelly family. Irishman Samuel Robert Kelly had been employed as a tram driver but was badly injured in an accident making it impossible for him to continue in his current employment. It was a worrying time for Samuel as he had a wife, Matilda, and four small children to provide for. Samuel had been paid compensation for his injury but needed to make a decision on what his future career should be and while reflecting on this problem he found himself drawn towards the eel and pie trade which was proving a great success in the area.

In 1915 Samuel Robert Kelly and his wife Matilda (who incidentally had been a Cooke before her marriage to Samuel) opened their first shop at 468 Bethnal Green Road. Matilda ran the shop each day whilst Samuel dealt with the ordering of the daily provisions of the trade. The Kelly's four children, Samuel, George, Matilda and Joe all joined their parents in the business and by the 1940s all four of the

Kelly children had opened shops. George's first shop was at 236 Roman Road, E3, then he opened a further shop at 56 Devons Road, E3. His brother Samuel opened a shop at 284 Bethnal Green Road (this shop is now run by his son Robert and will eventually pass to Robert's son Neil).

S Kelly 284 Bethnal Green Road c1915

S & R Kelly & Sons 2016   Robert Kelly 2016

Youngest brother Joe and their sister Matilda opened a shop together at 209 Green Street, E2, (now Roman Road) under the name of Kelly and Searle (Matilda's married name). George acquired two more shops the first at 600, then another at 526 Roman Road bringing the total number of shops owned by the Kelly family to seven with five of these iconic shops being sited within a mile and a half radius.

When the trade first started eel sales were of greater prominence than pies. You would often see a stall selling eels outside one of the Kelly shops. The eels themselves would be delivered fresh from the eel yard in Viaduct Street, Bethnal Green which was owned by George Kelly. Gradually the shops became very well known for their delicious eels, pies and mash with the, by now famous, green liquor.

All the shops were distinctive with marble topped tables and white tiled walls. I cannot speak for all of the shops but in the front window of S & R Kelly's shop in Bethnal Green Road, you can see the original shiny steel liquor containers that are still in use today.

Both world wars were to impact on the eel, pie and mash trades. At the start of each of these conflicts many of their male customers disappeared, either voluntarily or more likely through conscription into the armed services. As if this was not bad enough – the Government then introduced rationing. Many of the eel, pie and mash shops might have gone out of business but for their fame in providing good quality, reasonably priced meals for the working classes.

During World War Two, Bill Kelly, worried that his business might fail if he could not get supplies, decided to take his plight to the Ministry of Food and was given rations to continue his trade once he had pointed out that he was feeding the working classes. Another change brought about by World War Two was the death of the eel pie: the scarcity of eels during the conflict led to them being taken off the menu and they never really went back on although jellied and stewed eels returned to favour with the return of the men from war and the shops found themselves reaping the financial rewards of all the returning customers. This windfall was short lived though as many families moved out of the area in the 1950-60s to the new 'garden cities'. With the decline in trade, inevitably shops did close but there are enough of these about for those who still enjoy this famous, nutritious fare and long may that be the case.

One final mention of eels has to be the - by now locally famous -'Tubby' Issac's jellied eel stall on the corner of Goulston Street, Whitechapel – where Spitalfields meets with Aldgate. The business began in 1919 on what had once been the site of a snuff house (from one pungent smell to another methinks): over the years among the many customers who sought out the stall were some very famous actors of their time such as Lawrence Olivier and Vivian Leigh. Tubby successfully ran the stall until 1939 when he emigrated to America in an attempt to avoid his sons being conscripted into the services at the start of World War Two – but he could have stayed here as his sons were instead conscripted into the American armed forces. His nephew Solly ran the stall for many years following Tubby and his family departing these shores.

With a large Jewish population living and working in East London it is hardly surprising that kosher food establishments were opened and none more famous than Bloom's. Sidney Bloom opened his restaurant in 1920 in Brick Lane but moved to Whitechapel Road after World War Two. It was celebrated both for its food and its 'rude' waiters; people from all walks of life visited the restaurant including the Marx Brothers, Princess Margaret, Golda Meir; and Charlie Chaplin – and all were treated the same – standing in a queue and waiting to be served by a rude waiter. Yes, they really were rude but that was part of the experience! Sidney Bloom, famous for penny-pinching, required the waiters to 'buy' each meal for the customers from the kitchen and the staff would then earn commission on what they sold. With this ungenerous means of earning a living the waiters were understandably rather brusque - "sit there and wait until I am ready" would be the instruction barked at the customer and so the 'experience' would progress along the same lines until the bill was slammed down in front of the down-trodden customer. The only person to have avoided standing in a queue was Frank Sinatra who ordered a special delivery to his suite at the Savoy. Sidney Bloom, impressed with the order arranged, for it to be delivered on silver plates but to his horror the silverware was never returned – although Mr Sinatra did apparently enjoy the food.

Finally, though by no means least, on this multi-cultural feast is Pellicci's: the Italian café-restaurant at 332 Bethnal Green Road. The family travelled from Tuscany, Italy to live and work in Britain. They set up their business in 1920 and lived above their shop where their second youngest child was born in 1925. All the brothers worked in the café for a while, then the eldest son decided to open his own establishment in Barnet. In 1962 a new member of staff started work in the café and eventually married one of the brothers – Nevio; the couple had two children, Anna and Nevio Jnr who eventually joined the rest of the family working at the café. When I called in to meet Anna and Nevio to hear the history of the café I learned that their mother Maria is still working in the kitchens - cooking and from personal experience I can recommend the food – especially the bread pudding.

It is a wonderfully warm and friendly place to dine and I am sure this has always been the case. The art deco interior still has the original beautiful wood panelling on the walls and floor with, in-between the panelling, mirrors in the same art deco style and historic photos of various family members looking down on you. One local told me it is not so much a café more of a 'Befnal' Green institution and I think that sums it up rather nicely.

Pellicci's exterior 2016

22

Public Houses, Temperance
and Entertainment

No history of the area would be complete without a final
stroll around Bethnal Green to discover its entertainment
history so I will mention here some of the past times enjoyed
by the locals over the years, as many of these have and still do
play a very important part in everyday Bethnal Green life. I
have gone back in time a little to when some of the public
houses first came into being in order to give the reader a proper
history of these places.

Life in Bethnal Green as in most of the East End could often
be a tough, harsh existence and maybe that is why people from
the area had such a profound love of entertainment in its
various forms, perhaps perceived as an escape from the
drabness of life.

One of the most famous forms of 'entertainment' was of
course the many public houses in the area. The brewing of beer
is an ancient trade which had often in the past been carried out
by individuals or members of a family but as time went by
these small trades were taken over by companies. As
mentioned in an earlier chapter, several famous breweries
were based in and around the area, employing many locals in
the brewing and delivery of their products such as mentioned
before, my grandfather, James Overy, employed for many
years by Charrington as a drayman.

In an earlier chapter I mentioned the *Approach Tavern* in

Approach Road, but as you walk around the district, seeing just a few of the many public houses provides an insight into the other side of life for the locals. There are many famous public houses and although I am not going to mention all of them here, I am including one of the oldest public houses in the area: *The Old George* in Bethnal Green Road. The original public house was built in 1742 and was no doubt named for King George II. The account book of Truman, Hanbury and Buxton lists *The Old George* as taking receipt of beer from them that year. The public house still proudly stands today. On the corner of Cambridge Heath Road and Bethnal Green Road can be found probably the most famous public house in Bethnal Green: *The Salmon and Ball*. It is believed that it was named thus because of the 'Salmon' freely caught in the Thames and the 'Ball' being either a reminder of the Roman Emperor Constantine The Great or possibly a Huguenot link as the silk weavers' symbol was also a ball. Wherever the name was derived from, the reason for its fame was the hanging of John Doyle, an Irishman and John Valline of Huguenot descent, at the crossroads outside the pub. The two men's crime was cutting silk from the looms whilst on strike for higher wages although the actual charges they were found guilty of was rioting and machine breaking. On the previous page I have included a recent photo of this public house. It is still a traditional public house today and very popular with local people.

Often public houses would be named for a famous person, such as the *Marquis of Cornwallis* on the corner of Bethnal Green Road and Vallance Road but occasionally the name of the public house would be derived from a popular pastime such as bird keeping, first popularised by the Huguenots. *The Bird Cage* in Columbia Road is one such public house and although not the original building it is one that has stood on this site since 1760.

I mentioned in an earlier chapter that Ted Bates worked part-time in a public house. He used to help his cousin-in-law Alice, widow of Alfred Nelson and licensee of the *Jack Russell* pub in Green Street, Bethnal Green. The pub survived the *Blitz* but was sadly demolished in later years. During World War Two, Ted also worked part-time at *The Dundee Arms* in Cambridge Heath Road, Bethnal Green; in fact following one bombing raid he had to be pulled out of the rubble. His mother's family, the Durrell's, had been publicans and it had always been Ted's ambition to run his own pub but sadly he never fulfilled his dream.

Last but not least is a public house named for the Blind Beggar from which the badge of Bethnal Green was derived. The full story of the *Blind Beggar* can be found in the Foreword of this book. Stephen Sanders noted that often publicans in the area were in some ways the closest that Bethnal Green got to gentry in the 19th and 20th Centuries.

The people of Bethnal Green, as did locals in other parts of East London, enjoyed the social aspect of life whenever they were able. This does not mean to say that everyone was indulging in just a quick half pint on their way home from work. For centuries the public house was a means of escape from the grinding poverty of life for many unskilled men who were only able to obtain irregular employment. Indeed, much badly needed earnings would often be spent partially or even totally in a public house rather than providing food for the family. This does not mean that all men would succumb to regular drunkenness but before World War Two it was more common for a man to regularly frequent his local. In earlier centuries the public house was often the scene of many society meetings, in fact many of the early Huguenot immigrants' meetings in their local public house resulted in the founding of some of our well known friendly societies, thus paving the way for insuring against illness by paying a small premium into the society on a regular basis.

In the 19th Century, hardship and privation could often be the cost to the family if the head of the household chose to sometimes ignore his family's needs for his own. Indeed, a woman begging her husband not to spend his wages on drink as he entered his local was witnessed by Fredrick Charrington, a member of the Charrington brewing family who was shocked that his family's wealth was derived from the misery of others. This incident was to have a profound effect upon his life as he, and many others, tried to bring 'temperance' into the lives of many at that time.

By the mid-20th Century the public house was also a frequent meeting place for women where often they would meet to exchange local gossip. My mother recalled her stepmother-in-law would sometimes meet her friends in the pub to exchange gossip while, for example, shelling peas. During World War Two the pub also became a popular meeting place for soldiers' home on leave to meet their friends and family as often the 'leave' time would be brief. Frequently tunes could be heard wafting from doors opening into public houses as either a paid pianist or often a 'local' would play a selection of requests on the old 'Joanna' (piano). Ted, my dad said if you could knock out a few tunes on the piano you would never need any beer money.

One of the most iconic forms of entertainment associated with East London was the Music Hall. Although this form of entertainment was found elsewhere in the country it was first associated with this area. The Music Hall had evolved from earlier forms of entertainment (and I use the term 'entertainment' rather loosely here) which would today be socially unacceptable: for example John Merrick (known as the Elephant Man due to his acute physical deformities) was regularly paraded as 'Entertainment' until Dr Fredrick Treves, from The London Hospital, found him in 1884 and rescued him from such cruel exploitation. Historically, the *Penny Gaffs* were the forerunner of the Music Hall, with the entertainment being provided in, for example, disused stables opening onto the streets. There would be a wide ranging selection of amusement at these venues as diverse as one act of a Shakespearean play to blacked-up minstrels. The Penny Gaffs died out at the end of the 19th Century with the advent of new fire regulations and health and safety rules.

Music halls provided a variety of acts to delight the paying public. An article in the *Hackney Gazette* dated 16 February 1956 records there being many small music halls such as *The Baxendale* in Columbia Road and *The Forresters* in Cambridge Heath Road (which later became a Gaumont cinema).

Amongst the many famous artists of the late 19th and early 20th Century was Marie Lloyd who had been born in East

London. The people of Bethnal Green used to often attend the famous *Hackney Empire* (many of the well-known music halls have now gone but this one still survives though not as a music hall). The oldest survivor in the world is *Wilton's Music Hall* which was opened in 1888 in Graces Alley E1 and although the building has been used for a variety of other purposes since, including as a rag factory, it has now returned to its original use and is still offering quality entertainment today.

I often wondered what the difference between a theatre and a music hall was – apparently in a theatre you sit in rows of seats for the performance whereas a music hall used to offer you the chance to sit in groups at a table where you would, in that era, be allowed to drink and smoke.

Jack Stephens (Stephen Sanders' grandfather) grew up in Spitalfields (on the west side of Bethnal Green), and as a boy he would sell rotten fruit to people queuing outside the music halls – for them to throw at the acts if they were not to their liking.

There were other venues within the borough offering a variety of entertainment, for example Oxford House where events such as talent contests were often staged. Speaking of Oxford House (also mentioned in earlier chapters), the organisation hosted more than 'events': they supported wider activities included boys' clubs and societies (where families met resulting in individuals forming lifelong friendships). But Oxford House clubs imposed a strict ban on betting and beer, possibly narrowing membership!

Finally, a mention here of a sporting occasion enjoyed by spectators and participants alike, one that was and still is firmly fixed in the East End psyche – boxing. Repton Boxing Club in Cheshire Street and York Hall (mentioned in an earlier chapter) were renowned venues for boxing events. York Hall is still the venue for many boxing matches and claims to be 'the finest boxing club in England'. The club is near to

Paradise Row where the very famous boxer Daniel Mendoza lived for many years in the 18th Century, and today there is a blue plaque proudly displayed on the property to say when he lived there.

From just before the outbreak of World War Two, dancing became a favourite pastime with young people who frequented Hackney Town Hall, Leyton Baths (in the winter months it was converted to a dance hall), Hammersmith Palais (where Susie and John met for the first time) or even the Lyceum on the Strand.

I could mention many other social activities which were popular at different times with the people of Bethnal Green but one final popular social outlet in the first half of the 20th Century I will mention was the cinema. Bethnal Green's first cinema was *Smarts Picture Palace* at 281-285 Bethnal Green Road. The cinema had been built in 1912 and opened in April 1913. Then in late 1938, following renovation, it was re-opened and re-named *The Rex* until 1949 when it was taken over by the Essoldo group of cinemas and re-named *Essoldo* until it closed in 1964. My dad recalled as a boy excitedly queuing with his cousins for the Saturday morning matinee – often at least one of the group of children would duck down out of sight of the ticket seller behind the desk and get in for free if they did not have enough money to pay for all of the tickets – a common rouse I was informed.

This journey has been a pleasure to undertake. It is hoped the book will help guide you, the reader, through a century of change in Bethnal Green. The author hopes the book will enrich the knowledge of all readers, who may gain as much pleasure from the reading as the author obtained in the writing. The generations departed have left a legacy for us all. Members of the old families and new arrivals will certainly continue to thrive. Although Londoners including the present

Bethnal Greeners lead their lives as the present generation, in time... all depart. In a sense though all who pass by are still there in their legacy.

The older generations live on a little in this book, perhaps the present generation who read this book, indeed all who wander through the contemporary streets will reflect on the many features which have gone, together with the people. The book, in a small way, is an attempt to ensure that something of the recent past is not forgotten – people and places both.

So, present Bethnal Greeners and passing folk on your many ways from here to there perhaps pause a moment and think of those who once lived in the area and helped shape the history of Bethnal Green even as their very presence builds a new inheritance for those unknowns who surely shall follow.

Postscript
Stairway to Heaven Memorial

Since writing this book the work of fundraising has continued and will endure even after the Memorial is finally completed. This is to cover the cost of expenses such as routine maintenance work and the annual overheads for the Memorial Service in March at which family, friends and those of the wider community come together to pay their respects and to remember those who died. Many fund raising events have taken place since I started to write this book involving individuals from all walks of life as well as organisations and businesses whose common goal is to see a fitting Memorial for the 173 men, women and children who died that night. These include book signings at a local bookshop, a Pie and Mash centenary celebration, raffles of a print by a famous artist and football memorabilia; historic walks as well as the famous 'bucket' collections that were often attended by Pearly Kings and Queens who added their own colourful and cheery touch to the fundraising. There were also the more adventurous who took part in the London Marathon for several years as well as four young men who raised funds by completing the Ben Nevis challenge in 2015.

The Bethnal Green tube disaster is still the biggest civilian disaster in this country so please go to the link for the memorial website (as listed in the Acknowledgement section of this book) and read some of the poignant stories from people who lost loved ones or who witnessed the events of that terrible night

Joyce Hampton   **17 February 2016**

Appendix A

The Records of AB James Henry Norton

The author found James Norton's war record on the Imperial War Museum website and includes the following details as a tribute to the man, and his shipmates who gave their lives for their country. During World War Two many military records from World War One were destroyed by bombing.

First Name:	James Henry
Initials:	J H
Surname:	Norton
Age:	27
Nationality:	British
Date of Death:	24/01/1918
Information:	SON OF MR. AND MRS. JAMES NORTON, OF BETHNAL GREEN, LONDON, HUSBAND OF HARRIETT LOUISA NORTON, OF 49 APPROACH ROAD, BETHNAL GREEN.
Rank:	Able Seaman
Service No:	J/47559

Campaign Medals: Like many service personnel of World War One, James Henry Norton was entitled to the Victory Medal, also called the Inter Allied Victory Medal. This medal was awarded to all who received the 1914 Star or 1914-15 Star and, with certain exceptions, to those who received the British War Medal. It was never awarded alone. These three medals were sometimes irreverently referred to as 'Pip, Squeak and Wilfred'. Eligibility for this award consisted of having been mobilised, fighting, having served in any of the theatres of operations, or at sea, between midnight 4/5 August, 1914, and midnight, 11/12 November, 1918.

Women who served in any of the various military organisations in a theatre of operations were also eligible. As with many Armed Forces personnel, James Henry Norton was entitled to the British War Medal for service in World War One. This British Empire campaign medal was issued for services between 5 August 1914 and 11 November 1918. The medal was automatically awarded in the event of death on active service before the completion of this period.

Service: Royal Navy
Ship: HM Motor Lighter No X6

The following is an extract from official records listing those men who died with James that night and how they died; I have highlighted the entry for James. Granny Norton never knew these details and I am glad she was spared the heartbreak of this knowledge. All were killed in the following action.

On 24 January 1918, *X6* and *X110* were being towed by HM Tug *Desire* when they were confronted by a German U Boat 2.5 miles off Filey. She sank the tug with gunfire and laid bombs on the two lighters, the citation does not make it clear if both were sunk. There are no casualties shown for *X110* but a DSM was awarded to PO Redman of *X110*, so perhaps the vessel was indeed saved.

The Casualty List for X 6 (Meaning Killed)

BARRABLE JOSEPH H. STOKER 1c (RFR B 9422) 269700 (Ch) Motor Lighter X 6 24-Jan-18 SUBMARINE ACTION
FINCH EDWARD A. P.O. 218969 (Ch) Motor Lighter X 6 24-Jan-18 SUBMARINE ACTION
FOX EDWARD A.B., Mercantile Marine Reserve 786972 Motor Lighter X 6 24-Jan-18 SUBMARINE ACTION
KEANE BARTHELY CHIEF STOKER (RFR A 3582) 153201

(Dev) Motor Lighter X 6 24-Jan-18 SUBMARINE ACTION
NORTON JAMES H. A.B. J 47559 (Ch) Motor Lighter X 6 24-Jan-18 SUBMARINE ACTION
ROGERCOFSKY LOUIS A.B., Mercantile Marine Reserve 811844 Motor Lighter X 6 24-Jan-18 SUBMARINE ACTION served as **STANDER,** LOUIS

The Casualty List for X110

We can find no notice of casualties for X110 but there is a citation for a **REDMAN** Charles PETTY OFFICER, who was awarded a Distinguished Service Medal for his gallantry for 'Action with Enemy Submarines'.

The Casualty List for DESIRE

ALDERSON LEVI B. E.R.A., RNR E B 403 DESIRE 24-Jan-18 SHIP LOSS
DABNER THOMAS J. A.B., Yard Craft, H.M. Dockyard Chatham Admiralty Civilian DESIRE 24-Jan-18 SHIP LOSS
ELLWOOD HERBERT W. STOKER 1c (RFR B 5057) **182002 DESIRE 24-Jan-18 SHIP LOSS**
FOSTER LEWIS F. MATE (Yard Craft), H.M. Dockyard, Chatham Admiralty Civilian DESIRE 24-Jan-18 SHIP LOSS
KEEN PERCY G. L/STOKER K 3608 (Ch) DESIRE 24-Jan-18 SHIP LOSS
PINK WILLIAM STOKER (Yard Craft), H.M. Dockyard Chatham Admiralty Civilian DESIRE 24-Jan-18 SHIP LOSS
SEAMER WILLIAM I. STOKER (Yard Craft) H.M. Dockyard Chatham Admiralty Civilian DESIRE 24-Jan-18 SHIP LOSS
TUCKER CHARLES T. L/STOKER (Yard Craft), H.M. Dockyard Chatham Admiralty Civilian DESIRE 24-Jan-18 SHIP LOSS
VAUGHAN CHARLES F.F. A.B. J 26880 (Ch) DESIRE 24-Jan-18 SHIP LOSS

WITTY JAMES L. SEAMAN, RNR D 1602 DESIRE 24-Jan-18
SHIP LOSS

Family Members - in order of appearance

John Harris (B: 1834 M: 1853 D:)
Husband of Susannah Harris
Susannah Harris nee Taylor (B: 1834 M: 1853 D:)
Wife of John Harris, mother of Susannah Norton nee Harris
Susannah Norton nee Harris (B: 1862 M: 1885 D: 1932)
Daughter of John and Susannah Harris, wife of James Norton
Annie Taylor (B: 1811 M: D:)
Mother of Susannah Taylor grandmother of Susannah Norton nee Harris
James Norton (B: 1860 M: 1885 D: 1938)
Husband of Susannah Harris, son of Alfred Norton and Margaret Norton nee Barfield
Maggie Overy nee Norton (B: 1889 M: 1913 D: 1929)
Wife of James Overy, mother of Edward James Henry Overy and Margaret Elizabeth Harriet Smith nee Overy
James Henry Norton Jnr. (B: 1891 M: 1915 D: 1918) *KIA at sea. Husband of Lydia Harriet Norton nee Woolcot, father of James 'Jimmy' Norton and Lydia Atkins nee Norton* **Lydie Bates** nee Norton (B: 1893 M: 1929 D: 1979)
Wife of Ted (Albert) Bates 2, mother of Susie Bates nee Cain
Elizabeth Bates nee Norton (B: 1896 M: 1916 D: 1928)
Wife of Ted (Albert) Bates (1), mother of Eddy 'Edmund', and Arthur 'Artie' Bates
Charlotte Goodwin nee Norton (B: 1899 M: 1925 D: 1988)
Wife of Leonard Goodwin, mother of Leonard Goodwin Jnr
James Overy (B: 1889 M: 1913/35D: 1964)
Husband of Maggie Norton (1) Husband of Lizzie Carter (2) father of Edward James Henry Overy and Margaret Elizabeth Harriet Smith nee Overy
James W Overy (B: 1914 M–D: 1914)
Eldest son of James and Maggie Overy
Margaret Elizabeth Harriet Smith nee Overy (B: 1915 M: 1938 D: 1997)

Wife of Bert John Smith, mother of Peter and Sheila Smith, sister of Edward James Henry Overy

Harriet Lydia Norton nee Woolcott (B: 1894 M: 1915 D: 1956)
Wife of James Norton (Jnr) ,mother of James 'Jimmy' Norton and Lydia Atkins nee Norton

Phoebe Mary Deeks nee Bates (B: 1896 M: 1917 D: 1961)
Wife of Charles Deeks, daughter of Albert Edward Bates and Mary Anne Durrell

Albert Edward Bates (B: 1865 M: 1889 D:)
Husband of Mary Anne Bates nee Durrell, father of Ted, Bill, Phoebe, Marie and Arthur Bates

Ted (Albert) E Bates (B: 1891 M: 1916/29 D: 1946) *Husband to (1) Elizabeth Norton   (2) Lydie Norton, father to Eddy and Artie Bates and Susie Cain nee Bates*

Bill Bates (B: 1894 M: D: 1969)
Son of Mary Anne Bates nee Durrell, Brother to Ted, Phoebe, Marie and Arthur Bates

Charles Deeks (B: 1890 M: 1917 D: 1954)
Husband of Phoebe Bates, father of Phoebe Kerridge nee Deeks and Victor Deeks

James Edward Norton (B:1916 M:-D:1934)
Son of James and Harriet Lydia Norton nee Woolcott, brother of Lydia Atkins nee Norton

Lydia Marie Atkins nee Norton (B: 1918 M: 1938 D: 2007) *Wife of George Atkins, mother of George Atkins Jnr.*

Edward James Henry Overy (B: 1918 M: 1946 D: 1990)
Husband of Vera Overy nee Parkes, father of Joyce Hampton, brother of Margaret Elizabeth Harriet Smith nee Overy **Phoebe**

Alice Kerridge nee Deeks (B: 1918 M: 1940 D: 2013)
Wife of Charles Fredrick Kerridge, mother of Victor Charles Kerridge

Mary Anne Bates nee Durrell (B: 1868 M: 1889 D: 1908)
Wife of Albert E Bates, mother of Phoebe, Marie, Ted, Arthur and Bill Bates

Albert Edward Bates (B: 1920 M: 1950 D: 1969)
Husband of Janet Ewan, son of Elizabeth and Ted Bates, father of Janice Drewett

Joyce Irene Deeks nee Devey (B: M: 1947 D: 2014)
Wife of Vic Deeks, mother of Gloria Parker

Jenny 'Jane' Overy nee Reed (B: 1896 M: 1918 D: 1953)
Wife of Walter Overy, sister-in-law to James Overy, mother of Walter Stanley and Leonard William Overy
Walter Overy (B: 1896 M: 1918 D: 1950)
Husband of Jenny Overy, father of Walter Stanley and Leonard William Overy
Walter Stanley Overy Jnr. (B: 1920 M: D: 1962)
Eldest son of Walter and Jenny Overy
Leonard William Overy (B: 1925 M: D1999)
Youngest son of Walter and Jenny Overy
Sheila M Crates nee Smith (B: 1950 M: 1974 D:)
Daughter of Bert and Margaret Smith, sister of Peter Smith
Susie Cain nee Bates (B: 1931 M: 1958 D: 2007)
Wife of John Cain, daughter of Lydie and Ted Bates
Leonard Goodwin (B: M: 1925 D: 1986)
Husband of Charlotte Norton, father of Leonard Goodwin Jnr.
Arthur 'Artie' Bates (B: 1926 M: 1952 D: 1974) *Husband to Marcie Peters, son of Elizabeth and Ted Bates and father of Rayna Bates*
Leonard J Goodwin Jnr. (B: 1926 M: 1951 D:)
Son of Leonard Goodwin and Charlotte Goodwin nee Norton
Victor Charles Albert Deeks (B: 1929 M: 1947 D: 2006)
Husband to Joyce Irene Devey, son of Phoebe and Charles Deeks, Father of Gloria Parker
Albert 'Bert' John Smith (B: 1912 M: 1938 D: 1992)
Husband of Margaret Elizabeth Harriet Overy, father of Peter Smith and Sheila Crates nee Smith
Elizabeth 'Lizzie' Overy nee Carter (B: M: 1935 D: 1967)
Wife to (2) James Overy
John Deeks (B: 1915 M:1936 D: 1976)
Husband of Rose Ellis, father of Barbara Deeks (later Windsor)
Rose Ellis (B: 1912 M:1936 D ?)
Wife of John Deeks, mother of Barbara Deeks (Windsor)
Barbara Deeks (later Barbara Windsor MBE 2000; Freedom of City of London 2010) *(B:1937 M: 3 spouses; D:)*
Daughter of John and Rose Deeks
George J Atkins (B: 1917 M: 1938 D: 1981)
Husband of Lydia M Norton, father of George Atkins Jnr.
Granny Overy (Emma Deighter) (B: 1859 M: 1876 D: 1940)

Mother of James, Walter and 8 more children, grandmother of Margaret and Ted Overy

Vera Overy nee Parkes (B: 1920 M: 1946 D:)

Wife of Edward James Henry and mother of Joyce Hampton nee Overy

Mrs Kerridge (Snr.) nee Beach (B: M: D:)

Phoebe Kerridge's mother in law, mother of Charles Fredrick Kerridge

Arthur Stanley Bates (B: M: D:1943)

Son of Mary Anne Bates nee Durrell, Brother to Ted, Phoebe, Marie and Bill Bates

John Ewan (B: M: D:)

Brother of Janet Bates nee Ewan

Janet Bates nee Ewan (B: M: 1950 D: 1997)

Wife of Eddy Bates, mother of Janice Bates

Gloria Parker nee Deeks (B: 1949 M: 1984 D:)

Daughter of Vic and Joyce Deeks

Marie Phoebe Lilian Sanders nee Stephens (B:1925 M: D: 2013)

Cousin of Phoebe Kerridge

Peter Smith (B: 1945 M: 1971 D:)

Son of Bert and Margaret Smith, brother of Sheila Crates nee Smith

George J Atkins Jnr. (B:1939 M: D:2012)

Son of George Atkins and Lydia Norton nee Bates

Charles Fredrick Kerridge *(B:1916 M:1940 D:1983)*

Husband of Phoebe Alice Deeks, father of Victor Charles Deeks

Victor Charles Deeks (B:1943 M:- D:1960)

Son of Phoebe and Charles Kerridge

Marcella 'Marcie' Bates nee Peters (B: 1926 M: 1952 D: 2013)

Wife of 'Artie' Bates, mother of Rayna Bates

Joyce Hampton nee Overy (B: 1950 M: 1974/2004 D:)

Daughter of Ted and Vera Overy

John 'Jack' Thomas Stephens (B:1901 M: D: 1981)

Grandfather of Stephen Sanders and father of Marie Sanders

John Cain (B: 1929 M: 1958 D: 2009)

Husband of Susie Cain nee Bates

Janice Drewett nee Bates (B: 1957 M: 1986 D:)

Daughter of Eddy and Janet Bates

Rayna Bates (B:1961 M:-D:2003)
Daughter of Artie and Marcie Bates
Alice Nelson (B: 1890 M: D: 1946)
Widow of Alfred Nelson, cousin-in-law of Ted Bates
Alfred Nelson (B: 1890 M: D: 1937)
Husband of Alice Nelson, cousin of Ted Bates

Select Bibliography

(Note: I have included some web URLs for the use of students of the subject. But I must sound a note of caution because such sites may change an address detail and thus may be no longer accurate as depicted here. On the whole Internet sites have been used for confirmation and are of secondary status as source material.)

Chapter 1
Girling B. **Images of London: East End Neighbourhoods** Tempus Publishing 2005
Haines G. **Images of London: Bethnal Green** The History Press, Stroud 2004
Marriott J. **Beyond The Tower: A History of London** Yale University Press 2011
Kiple K. **Plague, Pox and Pestilence** Weinfeld & Nicolson 1997
Gordon D. **The Little Book of the East End** The History Press, Stroud 2010
A Topography of Tower Hamlets – courtesy Tower Hamlets Archive
East End Neighbourhoods page 111 www.british-history.ac.uk/report.aspx?com pg 2 of 13 http:/www.british-history.ac.uk/report   Public services page 3 Building and Social Conditions from 1876 to 1914 http://www.intriguing-history.com/education-acts-of-tough-on-poorfamilies
Life and Labour of the People in London Vol 4 pages 37,38 David Perdue's Charles Dickens Page – Dickens London
http://www.20thcenturylondon.org.uk/public-baths-and-laundries
http://www.spa-london.org/history-of-the-east-london-spa
http:/www.actionforchildren.org.uk
Document relating to formation of Children's Home
Reminiscences of Bonner Road – Courtesy of Tower Hamlets Archive

Chapter 2
Marriott J. **Beyond The Tower: A History of London** Yale University Press 2011
Life and Labour of the People in London Vol 5 page 182

Chapter 3
www.ppu.org.uk/learn/infodocs/people/pst_dick.html

Chapter 4
Author unknown. The Story of 25 Eventful Years in Pictures Odham Press Ltd 1935

Marriott J. Beyond The Tower: A History of London Yale University Press 2011

Unknown Author. In Flanders Fields: Museum Guide Watermill Books 1998

Cox J. Old East Enders: A History of The Tower Hamlets The History Press, Stroud 2013 **East London Observer**
http://www.historylearningsite.co.uk/rationing_and_world_war_one.
htm http:/ww1facts.net/war-at-sea/ww1-ships Britain during WW1 – Tower Hamlets Archive
London Illustrated News
Flight Magazine online
Postcards of the month – WW1 Bombing of Allen & Handbury

Chapter 5
Cox J. Old East Enders: A History of The Tower Hamlets The History Press, Stroud 2013
OU The Dogs of Alcibadies

Chapter 6
Kiple K. Plague, Pox and Pestilence Weinfeld & Nicolson 1997

Chapter 7
www.thch.org.uk/**UsefulInformation**/Publications/Hop...

Chapter 8
Cox J. Old East Enders: A History of The Tower Hamlets The History Press, Stroud 2013 www.british-history.ac.uk l
http://.jewisheastend.com/fourpercentdwellings.html The Bethnal Green and East London Housing Association

Chapter 9
Gordon D. **The Little Book of the East End** The History Press, Stroud
2010 http://www.igg.org.ul/gangsg/00-app1/trades-st.htm
http://www.victorianweb.org/history/work/costermonger.html

Chapter 10
Glinnert E. **East End Chronicles** Penguin Books 2006

Chapter 11
Houghton D. **A Bethnal Green Memoir** The History Press, Stroud 2009
**Special Report on an Outbreak of Typhoid Fever in the Borough of
Bethnal Green in 1924** by Geoffrey Eugene Oates.
http:bethnalgreeninfocus.org/tag/wash-houses/

Chapter 12
Nil

Chapter 13
Marriott J. **Beyond The Tower: A History of London** Yale University
Press 2011
Seaman L.C.V. **Post Victorian Britain 1902-1951** Methuen & Co,
London 1966
Glinnert E. **East End Chronicles** Penguin Books 2006
Lewis J. E. **London The Autobiography** Constable & Robinson,
London 2010
http://history-world.org/great_depression.htm http://spartacus-
educational.com/GERantisemitism.htm
www.british-history.ac.uk
Principles of the Bethnal Green Housing Assoc – Appeal to Christian
People

Chapter 14
Nil

Chapter 15
Marriott J. **Beyond The Tower: A History of London** Yale University
Press 2011

Seaman L.C.V. **Post Victorian Britain 1902-1951** Methuen & Co, London 1966

Glinnert E. **East End Chronicles** Penguin Books 2006

Lewis J. E. **London The Autobiography** Constable & Robinson, London 2010

http://history-world.org/great_depression.htm http://spartacus-educational.com/GERantisemitism.htm

www.british-history.ac.uk

Principles of the Bethnal Green Housing Assoc – Appeal to Christian People

Chapter 16

Grummet A. **History of St Matthew's Church Bethnal Green** St Matthew's Parochial Church Council date unknown

Healey T. **Life on the Home Front** Readers Digest Assoc. Ltd. 1963

Marriott J. **Beyond The Tower: A History of London** Yale University Press 2011 http:/bombsight.org/explore/greater-london/towerhamlets/bethnal-green

http://www.bbc.co.uk/history/british/britain_wwtwo/christmas_under_fire_01.shtml

Chapter 17

Houghton D. **A Bethnal Green Memoir** The History Press, Stroud 2009

Haines G. **Images of London: Bethnal Green** The History Press, Stroud 2004

Hackney Gazette 20th and 25th March 1942 copies taken of originals held by Tower Hamlets Archive

http://www.history.ac.uk/ihr/Focus/War/londonRation.html

http://www.museumofchildhood.org.uk/about-us/history-of-the-museum

Chapter 18

http://www.stairwaytoheavenmemorial.org

BBC Archive List WW2 People at War The Bethnal Green Tube Disaster

The National Archives Extracts of the Dunne Report

Chapter 19

Haines G. **Images of London: Bethnal Green** The History Press, Stroud 2004

Unknown Author **The Day War ended: Voices and Memories from 1945** Weindenfeld & Nicolson

Wilkinson L. **Watercress but no sandwiches: Three Hundred Years of the Columbia Road** Wilkinson 2001
http://scottbrownscerebralcaffeine.wordpress.com/tag/bethnal-total
missiles dropped on Bethnal Green

Chapter 20
Judt T. **Post War: A History of Europe since 1945** Pimlico, London 2007
Young M. & Willmott P. **Family and Kinship in East London** Penguin Books London 1957
Marriott J. **Beyond The Tower: A History of London** Yale University Press 2011
Glinnert E. **East End Chronicles** Penguin Books 2006
http://www.freerepublic.com/focus/fr/1757989/posts
http://www.bbc.co.uk/ahistoryoftheworld/objects
http://www.british-history.ac.uk/report

Chapter 21
Clunn C. Eels, Pie and Mash photographs by Chris Clunn
The Museum of London 1996
Gordon D. **The Little Book of the East End** The History Press, Stroud
Interviews with R Kelly of S & R Kelly: Nevio and Anna Pellicci
Pellicci's Café
http://estlondonhistory.com/2010/blooms-restaurant/
htt://www.historic-uk.com/CultureUK/Fish-Chips/
http://spitalfieldslife.com/2013/06/13/so-long-tubby-issacs-jellied-eels

Chapter 22
Glinnert E. **East End Chronicles** Penguin Books 2006
Haines G. **Images of London: Bethnal Green** The History Press, Stroud 2004
http://cinematreasures.org/theaters/16512

Throughout unpublished notes and records of conversations with family members and members of the public have been taken into consideration and informed the authors text.